The
RAINBOW NATION COOKERY GUIDE

Compiled by Pumla Brook -Thomae and Brent Abrahams

FIRST EDITION

ACKNOWLEDGEMENTS

Rotary eClub of Greater Cape Town
Design and layout: Wempic photography and design
Photography: Brent Abrahams
Artefacts: William Raats for the Zulu, Ndebele and Xhosa private collectables
The private collector for English artefacts
Recipes and stories: All the RNCG Chefs
The support team: Lynette Stassen
Dr Rainer Thomae
Mbasa Brook
Koos Myburgh
Juliet Mercia Adams

Copyright
ISBN number: 978-0-620--88774-8
ISBN Ebook number: 978-0-620-88775-5

Official website: www.rainbownationcooking.co.za

Photograph: UKHAMBA (beer pot) with decorative detail and typical black patina.

Contents

1	Zulu cuisine	9
2	Indian cuisine	18
3	Xhosa cuisine	25
4	Cape Malay cuisine	36
5	Afrikaans / Boere cuisine	48
6	The San/Xun way of life	56
7	Basotho cuisine	68
8	English cuisine	76
9	Tsonga cuisine	88
10	Northern Sotho Pedi cuisine	98
11	Ndebele cuisine	106
12	Swati cuisine	114

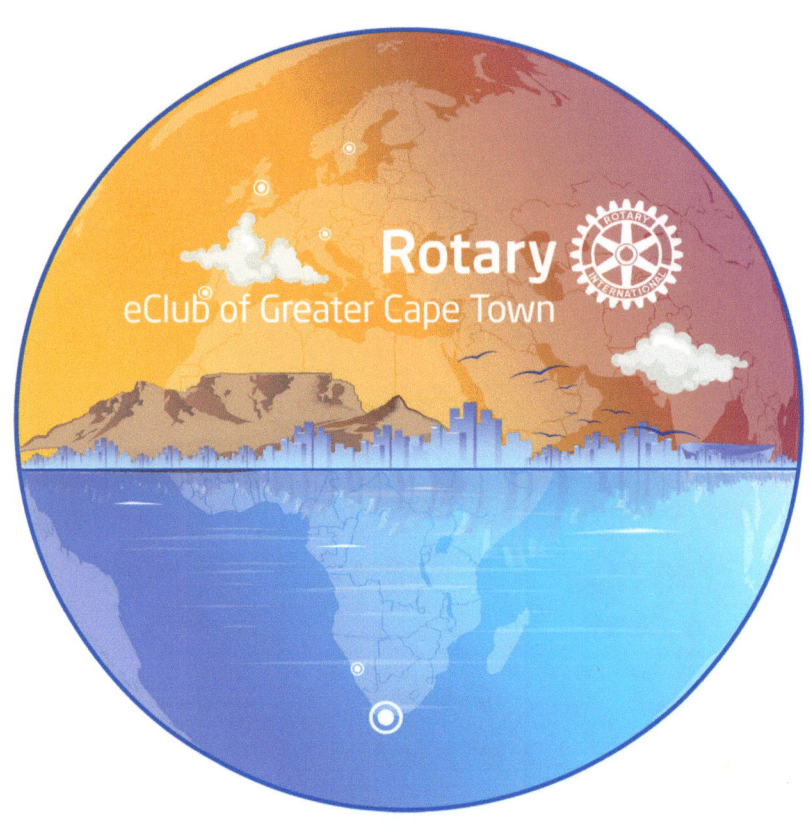

Rotary E-Club of Greater Cape Town

Why does our cookery guide refer to the Rainbow Nation? Because the title Rainbow Nation, captures the country's cultural and ethnic diversity.
This cookery guide adds to that colourful image by capturing the cultural cuisine of our South Africa population through the shared recipes of our 12 chefs from our South African cultures.

In the 1990s, the then Archbishop of Cape Town, Reverend Emeritus Desmond Mpilo Tutu, sometimes asked in big meetings: "Raise your hands". Then he said: "Move your hands". And then: "Look at your hands – the different colours representing different people. You are the Rainbow People…".

Our beloved President Nelson Rolihlahla Mandela loved that phrase and frequently described South Africa as the Rainbow Nation. One of his sayings that resonates with this book is that "each of us are infinity attached to the soil of this beautiful country like the jacaranda trees of Pretoria and the mimosa trees of the bushveld. A Rainbow Nation at peace with itself and the world."

The Rainbow Nation Cookery Guide is full of recipes to guide readers. It's not just read but also taste and enjoy the delights of cultural eating.

Happy reading; eating; learning and enjoying this unique cultural book with a difference.

Rainbow Hugs

Lynette Stassen

Lynette Stassen - President of the E-Club of Greater Cape Town 2021-2022.

Preface

By Pumla Brook-Thomae

Since I was a little girl, I have always found food to be fascinating. At age 13 I baked my first bread. Surprisingly, I ventured into acting; however food was still part of my life whether making it or talking about it, around family and in the public sphere. Recipe development, menu-making and cookbook writing seem to fulfil a hunger inside me.

After I published my first cookbook I really found my identity as a cook. My second cookbook - Family Food Simplified - is a book dedicated to my Mom and a homage to the dishes that I grew up eating. Only then did I discover my passion - simple family-style food that appeals to the South African palate, injected with global flavours. To pursue that I needed to go back to my roots. But culture does not exist in isolation and acknowledging other cultures were the way to go, while still learning about my own. I soon realised how little has been documented about South African foods both locally and on the global scene.

The Rainbow Nation Cookery Guide (RNCG) is the answer I was looking for. I'm certain I speak for many South Africans here. It offers an all-inclusive South African cookery guide which can be a blueprint for generations to come. A journey through our country, it features our unique cuisines and our diverse people. The RNCG is a quest to put South African foods on the global map, with the help of 11 different chefs who share their culture and food. This book preserves those authentic South African dishes which have nourished us for years. It gives them the respect they deserve. This book shows the world there is more to us as South Africans than our divided past – and what better way to do this than through food?

The RNCG is an epitome of simplicity. Some recipes require as few as two ingredients to make a meal. It really does not get any simpler than that. Yes you can expect foreign ingredients here and there but do not despair - a detailed South African glossary is provided to help you navigate this book with ease and substitutions are offered for those ingredients you might find difficult to source.

This cooking guide boasts a wholesome cooking experience catering for every dietary need. Most of the dishes are based on South Africa's popular staples such as grains, samp, maize-rice, maize meal or miliemiel, sorghum, groundnuts and rice. You can take comfort in dishes made with your regular favourite vegetables but expect exotic options as well, such as edible weeds. Umfino/morogo refers to a combination of edible weeds eaten as a side or used as a foundation for a lot of indigenous dishes.

For meat lovers, we have barbecued ribs, Sotho bashed beef and beef stew. We've got you covered with the ever popular Sunday roast chicken, free-range home-bred chicken and chicken curry.

For the meat-free eater, our vegetarian mains, sides and soups feature wild leaves such as pumpkin leaves, cassava leaves, morogo, legumes, bambara nuts, dried fruits and veggies. An array of dishes offering ample options so you do not miss out on great South African food.

For a more exotic experience, mopani worms are a delicacy from the Limpopo Province, amadumbe from King-Shaka Province and porcupine stomach from the San. The Bushman culture boasts recipes that not only nourish but which are believed to carry healing properties.

Maybe you have a sensitive gut and could use gut-friendly options. Well, I am excited to let you know this book is truly as all-inclusive as its title suggests. You can look forward to fermented options for breakfast, drinks and more.

Each chapter of this book offers a unique culinary experience from each of the featured cultures. But that is not all - some of the techniques that were used in the past are showcased in this book to give you a glimpse of just how far we have come as a Rainbow Nation.

I could go on and on but I'll leave it here for now. Enjoy the taste of South Africa on a plate. May it inspire you to read this book and learn more about my country. May the dishes presented in this book ignite your taste buds in unexpected ways because you were brave enough to try something new.

To all the chefs and cooks who contributed their recipes and shared their culinary journey in making this offering, I am forever grateful. Together we did it! Here's to our shared love for our Rainbow Nation Food!

> A fusion of cuisines, traditions, and crafts that has influenced our South African way of cooking.

Historical Zulu kitchen utensils: (1) ITUNGA (milk pail). (2) UKHAMBA (beer pot), beautifully decorated with a typical black patina. 3. IMBENGI (grass lid) with beadwork.

1 Zulu cuisine

Recipes inspired from the Kwa-Zulu Natal region.

With its rich history and culture, the Zulu nation is the most extensively represented in South Africa.

Some traditions are recognized worldwide, like the dance (indlamu) performed by Zulu men in their traditional attire. Their art and crafts, like their decorative woven grass baskets and clay beer vessels called ukhamba, are also sought after by international collectors.

Historically, Zulu people worked the land to sustain themselves and grew crops like maize (umbila). Maize still remains the foundation of most meals and popular Zulu beverages.

An example of one of the Zulu maize dishes is umdokwe, a porridge made from milled dry maize (impuphu). It is enjoyed for breakfast, sometimes with sugar and milk. It is also fermented to make a drinking porridge called amahewu.

Other traditional beverages include African beer called umqombothi. It is made from maize and brewed using traditional customs. These customs vary slightly between regions. Traditionally umqombothi is served in a clay beer pot called ukhamba. These clay vessels are examples of the design and decoration of food and beverage utensils in the Zulu culture. Design, just like methods of cooking, have evolved over the years.

The Zulu have a variety of methods to cook maize. These include freshly fire-roasted, boiled as a snack, or prepared as a porridge.

A crumbly and fluffy variation of cooked maize is called uphuthu. It is the mainstay of Zulu cuisine and is a dish that holds its own as a meal in one or as a side dish. Uphuthu has many variations, including adding beans to create isigwaqane.

Another variant to the recipe is adding pumpkin to make isijingi. A comforting, slightly sweet dish qualifying as a porridge but tasting pudding-like once sugar and butter are added.

Uphuthu is also often a side dish to many meat dishes such as isityu stew or wilted wild greens such as wild spinach (imbhuya).

There are many similarities between Zulu cuisine and Xhosa cuisine. Uphuthu namasi, like African maize beer, is an example of this.

Other staple foods include bread. The Zulu people traditionally make bread in various ways, like ujeqe, a steamed bread made from whole steamed flour and idombolo, flour bread steamed over a stew.

The Zulu nation prides itself on simple cooking techniques that produce tasty dishes. Their love for food and its preparation is also evident in their adorned historic utensils for food collection and preparation. Created from necessity, these have to become collectable works of art, many of which are still created today.

Chef Manqoba Langa has included some timeless Zulu recipes.

From the chef

Manqoba Langa

I was born in Kwa Zulu-Natal, also known as King Shaka Province. I grew up in a town called Ulundi City of Heritage in a small village called Mhlahlane. In our village, we grew almost everything we consumed.

I was raised by my granny from my mother's side. I stayed with her because my parents worked. Living with her was such a great time in my life, and I learned many life lessons such as sharing, respect and definitely cooking. Sadly, she passed away in 2004. I then moved to Johannesburg, in the province of Gauteng.

My love for food, therefore, comes from watching my grandma cook simple, comforting food. I was always in the kitchen when she was cooking. I was always the kitchen assistant. Getting what is needed, fetching water, providing the suitable mixing bowls to the passing on of the knife. It was something I enjoyed doing.

I later joined Hotel School and graduated in 2014 from the International Hotel School in Christina Martin Culinary Arts Institution in Johannesburg. After that, I worked for a few hotels in South Africa. Then, in October 2017, I was offered an opportunity to be part of the trainees at Hotel Fairmont in Texas Austin (USA). After completing my trainee program, I came back home to South Africa and worked as a freelancer.

In 2019 I joined the Princess Cruise Liner as a demi-chef de parte for a 9 months contract which meant another move, one that meant working at the sea.

You could say I have moved around a lot in my life, from granny in Kwa-Zulu Natal to Joburg, to around the world and even the sea, for that matter. These moves have shaped me into a person who can easily adapt to new places and workspaces.

To date, I was meant to make another move. I had been offered an inflight chef position in Saudi Arabia Airlines, which was suspended due to the outbreak of the Covid-19 pandemic. I am looking forward to what lies ahead culinary-wise and any lessons this move may bring when it finally happens.

Amadumbe   Umnyandu wezinkobe   Isigwaqane
Isityu senyama yenkomo   Isinkwa sombila

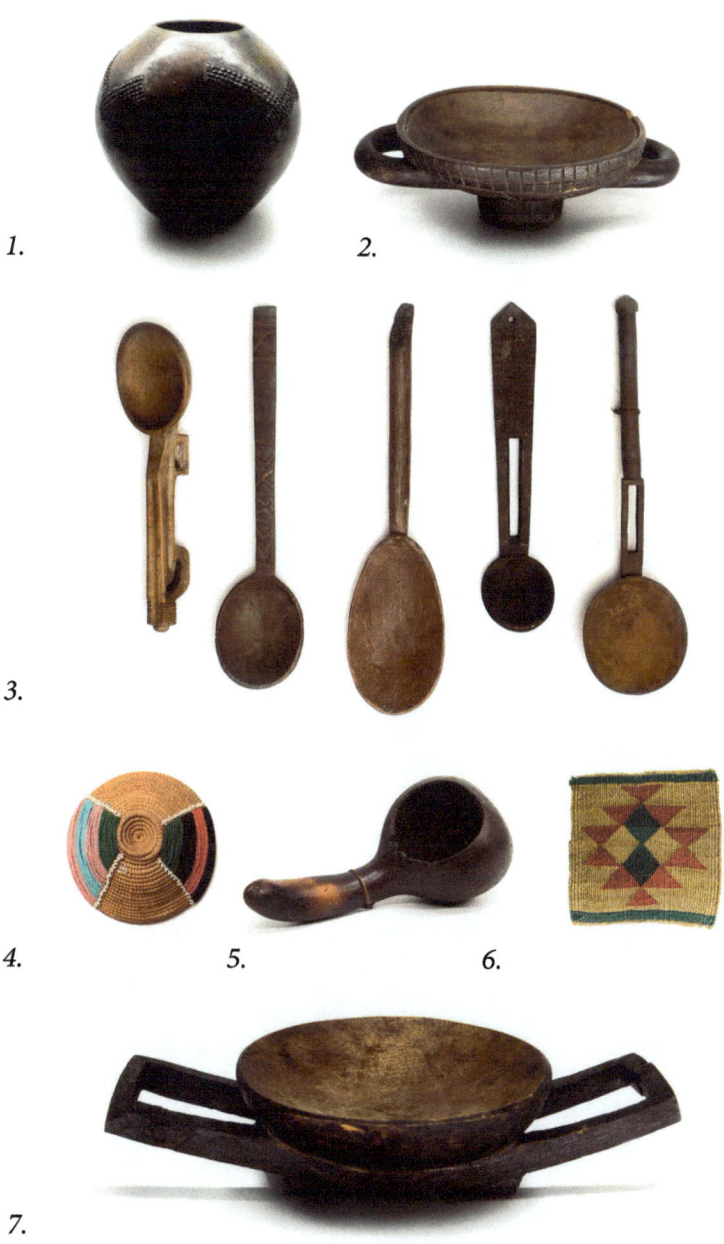

Historical handcrafted Zulu kitchenware: (1) UKHAMBA (beer pot). (2) UGQOKO (meat platter) handcrafted from wood with decorative detail. (3) IZINKHEZO (spoons) with decorative design. (4) IMBENGI (grass lid) with beadwork. (5) Calabash ladle. (6) Reed, woven place mats. (7) UGQOKO (meat platter) handcrafted from wood with decorative detail.

Amadumbe
potato of the tropics / colocasia esculenta

Amadumbe is a tuber or root vegetable similar to sweet potatoes and a cross between sweet potato and potatoes in flavour. They grow in the Kwa-Zulu Natal Province in the southeast part of South Africa.

The leaves slightly resemble that of butternut but much thicker, while the skin feels much rougher than potatoes. The edible parts are both the leaves and the root.

It is best enjoyed in its natural form in the Zulu culture by simply steaming or boiling it.

To prepare, scrub thoroughly and rinse off any sand and grit. Then, steam or boil with the skin on and only remove the skin before eating. Once cooked, amadumbe do tend to be mushy. A pot of water is all you need. It is a versatile vegetable that is often made into curries in this region.

Ingredients

500 ml water
500 g amadumbe

Bring a medium pot to a boil and gently simmer the amadumbes until a skewer can be inserted or a small knife cuts through without resisting. Cool slightly and enjoy.

Umnyandu wezinkobe
spinach and maize

Umnyandu is one of our village's favourite dishes, and it was traditionally made using preserved dried maize.

Ingredients

1 kg spinach
3 cups dried maize
1 onion chopped
salt to taste

Place the maize in a pot, cover with water and then cook until the maize is soft. Set it aside.
Blanch the spinach in hot water for 5 minutes, then take it out of the water and chop it into smaller pieces.

Sauté the onion, add the spinach, and continue to cook for a few minutes. Then add the maize and season to taste.

" Best enjoyed by simply steaming or boiling it."

Zulu cuisine: Amadumbe

Isiqwaqane (mielie and bean stiff porridge) served in a bowl on historical Zulu hand-woven placemats.

Isigwaqane
mielie and bean stiff porridge

Ingredients

1 cup sugar beans
1 ½ cup maize meal
1 tbsp cooking oil
1 tsp salt

Place the beans in a bowl, cover with boiling water and allow to soak overnight. The following day discard the water and rinse the beans until the fluid runs clear.

Place the beans in a pot, add warm or boiling water to the beans and place it on the stove to simmer on medium-low heat. Once tender, reduce the heat to low.

In a mixing bowl, mix the maize meal with water to a smooth porridge-like consistency. Then add the maize meal, cooking oil and salt to the beans. Stir until well combined. Cover the pot and gently steam for about 40 minutes, stirring every 10 minutes. Serve it hot.

Isityu senyama yenkomo
beef stew

Ingredients

2 kg stew beef cut into cubes
1 onion chopped
6 potatoes (medium)
salt to season
1 ½ litre water
2 tbsp oil

Traditionally the stew is cooked in a pot over a fire. However, the same technique applies to conventional cooking methods. Heat a pot on the stove until it is smoking hot, add the beef cubes and sear and seal the meat.

Add the chopped onion and sauté till golden brown. Season with salt.

Add 1 ½ litre of water then let it simmer for approximately 1 ½ hour.

Add the potatoes and cook for another half an hour until the potatoes are cooked through.
Add seasoning and serve.

Isinkwa sombila

steamed fresh corn (mielie) bread

This steamed cornbread was typically made daily and can only be made using fresh corn. The natural fluids of the corn assist in binding the ingredients and keeping the bread moist. No raising agents were used in the past. These days baking powder is added for a lighter loaf.

Ingredients

- 2 fresh corn cobs
- 4 cups of cake wheat flour
- 2 cups maize meal
- 4 teaspoons baking powder
- 2 tsp salt
- 2 cups luke-warm water
- 1 tsp oil or butter

Fill a pot a third of the way up with water and bring to a boil. While the water is simmering, start preparing the dough mixture.

Remove all the corn kernels from the cob and retain the husks for later use. Then grind the corn with a grinding stone, alternatively, roughly process the corn into smaller pieces.

In a mixing bowl, combine the ground corn, flour, baking powder, maize meal, salt, and water and mix into a pliable dough.

Lightly brush the inside of a stainless-steel bowl or microwave-safe glass bowl with oil or butter. Immerse the buttered bowl into a deep pot on top of the husks.

The husks will act as a barrier preventing the bowl from coming into direct contact with the heat. Cover the pot and gently steam until puffed up and doubled in size. It takes 1 ½ -2 hours to cook.

The bread is ready when a skewer or knife inserted comes out clean. Enjoy it as is or with beef stew (isityu senyama yenkomo).

Makes - 2 loaves

ISINKWA sombila (steamed fresh corn bread) with traditional hand-woven baskets.

2 *Indian cuisine*
Recipes inspired from the region of Kwa-Zulu Natal.

Indian cuisine is known to be spicy, aromatic, and flavourful. The result of cooking with classic spice combinations and a variety of cooking techniques. The tastes and cooking styles adopted and adapted locally influencing many dishes associated with South Africa. Biryani is an example and even popular street foods like "Bunny chow", also known as "Curry bunny".

In the mid-1800s, Indians arrived as indentured labourers and passengers from India's northern, southern and western parts. They brought with them traditional spices and used local ingredients to augment them. Over time, European and African ingredients were also added. The result, a distinctly South African flavour, not as spicy as it would have been in India.

Typically, dishes like Indian curries are made with vegetables or meat and served with rice. These are all prepared with a unique combination of spices (Masala). Masala is defined as a mixture of ground spices used in Indian cooking, like "Mother-in-law Masala".

They are "believed to awaken your senses" flavours of Indian cuisine has undoubtedly changed how South African food tastes and how we cook.
Khari Kitchri, a popular rice dish, is one of these flavourful recipes provided by Chef and spice extraordinaire, Fatima Seedat.

Indian cuisine: Grinding coriander with mortar and pestle, and spice selection.

From the chef

Fatima Seedat

I was born in Lenasia Johannesburg and I come from a long line of foodies. My mum was a renowned cook in our family. So our best family time was sitting around the kitchen table, laughing and enjoying my mother's delicious cooking.

I've had a varied career, starting as a trainee journalist in a community newspaper, working at a bank, working as a tourist guide, and an NGO that dealt in aquaculture, but my passion lies in business.

I am a businesswoman who has run different businesses throughout the years, but I found my calling in making spice. This business allows me to share the joy that food can bring to others and engage with people.

I value interacting with others. I also enjoy being my own boss, making my own decisions and pursuing my own vision.

There are two paths in my life, one following my entrepreneurial vision and the other is as a human rights activist. Human rights work is eradicating poverty and ensuring that people live a life with dignity and justice. This view was shaped by my experience as a student activist in the apartheid era.

I am part of an NGO called the Centre for Constitutional Values, which seeks to bring the constitution's values to life.

I am also an avid animal lover, particularly cats. I have two beautiful cats, who gives me immense comfort and joy.

I nominate Impilo Child Protection and Adoption Services, to receive any revenues which may be due from this project.

Lamb curry   Kitchri   Khari   Spicy spinach   Sweet butternut

Lamb curry, Kitchri and Khari yoghurt sauce. 21 *Indian cuisine*

Lamb curry

Ingredients

1 kg lamb leg pieces (fat trimmed and chopped into bite-size pieces)
4 tbsp oil
2 large onion finely chopped
2 tbsp ginger (crushed)
1 tbsp garlic crushed
¼ tsp nutmeg ground
2 cloves ground
1 ½ tsp salt to taste
½ tsp turmeric
1 tbsp ground cumin
1 tbsp ground coriander
1 lemon (juiced)
½ tsp whole cumin seeds
4 cinnamon sticks
4 cardamom pods
3 potatoes (cut into 3)
2 large tomatoes
200 ml yoghurt
1-1 ½ cup water
Fresh coriander for garnish

Marinate the lamb pieces with ginger, garlic, all dry spices and lemon juice. Then leave for 30 minutes.

Heat the oil in a pot and add the onions, cumin seeds, cinnamon sticks and cardamom pods. Fry the onions until light brown.

Add the meat with the marinade mixture to the pot and gently simmer for 30 minutes.

Add the potatoes and stir yoghurt into the mix. Add 1-1 ½ cup of water and cook until the meat and potatoes are soft.

Kitchri

spicy rice

Ingredients

¾ cup dhal (lentil)
2 cups rice
3 cinnamon sticks small
4 cardamom pods
½ tsp turmeric
1 tsp salt
1 tsp cumin seeds
2 tbsp ghee/clarified butter
3 cups water

Rinse the lentils and add 1 cup of boiling water. Let it soak until the lentils are slightly soft. Rinse again and transfer to a pot.

Add the rice, remaining water, salt, turmeric, cardamom and cinnamon sticks. Boil until soft.
Then steam rice/lentils until the rice is soft and fluffy.

Tempering

In a pan, melt the ghee/clarified butter and then add the cumin seeds. As soon as the cumin seeds begin to pop, remove them from the heat and then add the tempered seeds to the rice.

Khari
yoghurt sauce

Ingredients

500 ml double thick yoghurt
2 green chillies
handful of fresh coriander leaves
2 cloves of garlic
½ onion small
½ tomato
1 tbsp cake flour
salt
½ tsp cumin seeds
5 curry leaves
1 tbsp cooking oil

Blend all ingredients except for the oil, cumin and curry leaves until it is smooth.

Heat oil in a saucepan, add cumin and curry leaves. Once the cumin seeds pop, add the liquidised mixture and stir continuously.

Remove from heat once the mixture boils.
Serve with kitchri.

Spicy spinach

Ingredients

1 bunch spinach (any type)
2 tbs oil
½ tsp cumin
½ tsp mustard seeds black
½ onion small thinly sliced
¼ tsp turmeric
½ tsp salt
1 small tomato
2 garlic cloves

Add oil, mustard seeds and cumin to the pot with thinly sliced onion. Cook until golden brown.

Add the spinach, garlic, spices, salt and tomatoes. Simmer until the spinach is soft.
Serve as a side with kitchri.

Sweet butternut

Ingredients

1 butternut small
2 tbsp ghee/clarified butter
pinch of salt
1 tsp sugar
½ tsp garlic
½ tsp cinnamon ground
½ tsp chilli flakes

Dice the butternut.

Then melt the ghee in a pot and then add the spices and the diced butternut.

Stir to mix the ingredients and then steam until it cooks through.

The traditional Xhosa baskets woven from river reed (iingobozi) can be identified by their organic look with less decorative aspects when compared with other African weaving styles. Instead, the Xhosa baskets appeal is in the organic shape and form. These baskets are still produced and have evolved to become sought after interior pieces of design.

3 Xhosa cuisine

Recipes inspired from the regions of Eastern and Western Cape.

The Xhosa nation comes mainly from the Eastern Cape Province, Western Cape, and some spreading to Zimbabwe. Their pride and joy is utata, the "father" of the nation, the late former President of South Africa, Mr Nelson Rholihlahla Mandela. He was also the number one ambassador of Xhosa Cuisine.

Like many African cuisines, the staple foods and ingredients are similar with variations to dishes. The Xhosa staples also include fresh maize (umbhonomtsha), dried and crushed coarse grains (umngqusho), vegetables, wild edible greens, various bread and the amaXhosa favourite food, meat.

Traditionally the Xhosa prepare and cook food over a fire made with wood or dried cow dung (ubulongwe). Once the food is cooked, it is then allocated following a specific hierarchy. For example, male seniors are given premium cuts like brisket (ugeme) and cow and sheep's liver with lace fat (umhlehlo). In contrast, tripe (ulusu) is shared out with the women.

A quintessential of Xhosa cuisine is, (umngqusho onee mbhotyi), also known as samp and beans. It's a must-try recipe.

For the reader who may be unfamiliar with maize and samp products, maize, although often eaten fresh, is also dried, crushed and grinded to various degrees. These refined grains are used to create a variety of dishes. For example, a refined version of maize meal, combined with sorghum, is used for African beer (umqombhothi). Refined samp (umgrayo), a maize-rice, is used in making (umqa kajodo) by adding a melon called (umxoxozi).

Chef Pumla Brook-Thomae has included some of her Xhosa recipes.

From the chef

Pumla Brook-Thomae

My life experience, upbringing and circumstances have inspired me as a cook. They have equipped me to create tasty yet straightforward, cost-effective recipes that people enjoy.

I come from a big family. I'm the middle child of 7 children, and with my mom and dad, that makes a total of 9. So nine mouths to feed daily was my mom's everyday challenge. This challenge with ingredients that were never in abundance.

My dad was a qualified lawyer. However, he was refused the right to practise law by the then ruling party of the time. This was due to skin colour. So, out of desperation to provide for his family, he ended up working as a messenger at a bookshop.

My mom was the homemaker, and she also had to cook daily. With limited resources, she would combine ingredients and play around with flavours, all to prevent us from getting bored of the same foods.

On the plus side, living on a farm had its own perks. Our grandparents taught us about the food around us, the wild edible greens.

The thought of my grandmother always brings a smile to my face. She, holding my hand in the garden and teaching me the names of different weeds. She would give me a plastic bowl to help forage, and then she would place her harvest in her long skirt. These were our bonding moments.

I still remember how my grandmother made the most amazing dishes from these greens. One of these dishes is called umfino, a combination of wild leaves like dandelions (ihlaba), lamb's quarter (imbhikicane), pumpkin leaves (imithwane), and stinging nettle (irhawu/urhalijane). She also added the ever so controversial potato leaves. These were cooked till tender, and then a dose of maize meal would be added to complete the dish. It would be steamed and then enjoyed as a one-pot meal.

These are the memories and experiences that I carry with me and that has contributed to my career in food.

Umbhako   Isophu Amarhewu   Umngqusho onee mbhotyi   Umphokoqo onamasi

My contribution to my community can be experienced through my charity "PumlasFood Soup Kitchen." The self-funded initiative was founded to nourish unemployed men looking for jobs in the trade industry. These men, often found on street corners, are looking for work on an empty stomach.

One of my wishes by contributing to this cookery project is to use the proceeds to help my charity serve more people. The need has now increased with the Covid-19 pandemic and a high unemployment rate. Sadly, there are more people now who go to bed on an empty tummy.

Umbhako
pot bread

Umbhako or pot bread is also known as isonka sombhako in the urban areas of the Eastern Cape. Traditionally, the bread was baked over the coals in a flat cast iron pot with a lid and another layer of coals over the lid. This process mimicked an oven. These days, especially in urban areas, regular aluminium pots over electric or gas stoves are methods commonly used. As a result, baking over the fire has become a choice and is no longer a necessity.

The traditional way of cast iron pot baking still has its own character and adds a distinctive smoky flavour to the bread, unlike the conventional methods. However, there is a technique to baking over the coals. The bread is baked on low heat. Therefore there needs to be sufficient distance between the coals and the pot to prevent burning. Nowadays, a trivet can be used, but originally rocks served the same purpose.

Ingredients

1k g bread flour
2 ¼ active dried yeast
1 tbsp salt
2 tbsp white granulated sugar (optional)
650 ml luke-warm water
1 tbsp oil

Sift the flour, salt, yeast, and sugar into a mixing bowl. Add the water and mix into a soft but not sticky dough.

Cover the bowl with plastic wrap and then a tea towel. Place it in a warm place and leave it to rise. The dough will take approximately 1 ½ - 2 hours to double in size.

Once the dough has risen, knock the dough down and shape it into a round ball for about 10 seconds. Transfer into a large cast iron pot that has been lightly oiled on the inside and leave to rise for the second time. About 30 minutes.

The second rise makes for a fluffier, chewier bread. For a denser loaf omit the second rising and bake the bread after shaping it into a ball.

Place a trivet over the coals and then the pot over the trivet. Close the lid and place an even layer of coals over the cast pot's lid. Monitor the coals that they do not completely die out. Adding a little more at a time to ensure consistent heat throughout the baking process.

The bread is ready when it becomes fragrant and the top looks lightly golden. You would have to insert a skewer to check if it is done.

Once ready, remove the bread from the pot and then cover it with a clean tea towel. This will result in a softer crust. Alternatively, leave to cool on a cooling rack for a more crusty bread. Slather with butter and enjoy.

The traditional way of cast iron pot baking has it's own character and flavour.

Xhosa cuisine: Umbhako pot bread

Isophu
maize and bean soup

In the Xhosa culture, we technically don't have soups, although Isophu may be described as a soup of maize or corn cooked with beans. Peas are also used as an alternative to beans. It's a comforting and filling dish that needs no accompaniments.

Ingredients

250 ml sugar beans dried
250 ml maize dried
2 litres warm water
2 tbsp cooking oil
salt to taste

Rinse the beans and the maize until the water runs clear. Then cover the ingredients with 1 litre warm water and let them soak overnight.

The following day discard the soaking water and rinse again until the water runs clear.

Place the ingredients in a pot and add the remaining water. Simmer until tender. Then add the oil and season with salt. Serve it as a warm soup.

Amarhewu
fermented maize meal probiotic drink

Amarhewu, also known as inqodi, is the left-over maize meal porridge, left to ferment and used as the basis for a refreshing summer drink with probiotic benefits.
Its thick consistency results in a drink that is refreshing and substantial. It quenches thirst, fills the tummy and is gut-friendly. Providing a natural source of probiotics.
It was also my father's favourite drink and a beverage that we were never caught without on the farm.

Ingredients

500 ml maize meal
5 litre water
2 tsp flour
1 tsp sugar
¼ tsp yeast

Makes approximately 2,5 litres

Bring 400 ml of the water to a boil in a pot.

In a separate bowl, mix the maize meal with 500 ml of water and whisk until smooth.

Then add the maize mixture to the boiling water, whisking continuously to prevent lumps.
Reduce the heat and let it simmer until cooked into a thick porridge. This will take about 30 minutes. Once cooked, let the maize porridge cool completely.

Mix the flour, sugar and yeast with a bit of water, just enough to form a paste. Then add this mixture to the cooled porridge and mix well. Lastly, add the rest of the water and whisk until smooth.

At this stage, the mixture will resemble a thick porridge but will turn runnier and drinkable once fermented.

Transfer the mixture into a plastic container with a lid such as a bucket and store amarhewu until fermented. If making amarhewu during winter or cold days cover the container with a blanket. A technique used to encourage the fermentation process.

Once fermented, enjoy as is or with a bit of added sugar as a cooling drink.

In summer first fermentation will happen overnight, but an additional day is recommended for full fermentation. Totalling to 1 ½ days. The consistency should be that of drinking yoghurt.
During extreme cold fermentation will take longer than 1 ½ days. It may take up to 3 days.

Umngqusho onee mbhotyi
samp and beans

Umngqusho onee mbhotyi is one of those dishes that my mom and I bond over. It's also a dish that the Xhosa people hold dear to their hearts. Like many dishes, each family has their own variations of cooking umngqusho onee mbhotyi. This recipe is often adapted according to the tastes of the majority of the family rule.

When I was a child, my moms' ratio of beans and samp was 1:1 equal amounts of samp to the beans. The samp must be cooked through but still left with a bit of a bite and dense texture. Nowadays, my mom and I both prefer an alternative of butterbeans to the traditional sugar beans. Also, we add, and sometimes replace the beans with vegetables.

Ingredients

1 cup samp
1 cup sugar or butter beans
1 litre hot water
2 tbsp vegetable fat
½ beef stock cube (optional)
3 tsp white pepper (optional)
1 tsp salt

Place the samp and beans in a colander and rinse until the water runs clear. Place in a bowl and top with 1 litre boiling water. Cover it and leave to soak overnight or until it's doubled in volume.

The following day, first, discard all the soaking water and rinse the samp and beans off a few more times until the water runs clear.

Transfer the ingredients to a pot and top with 1-litre boiling water. Then simmer over medium heat for 1 hour until al dente. If you prefer softer samp, cook for 30 minutes longer.

Season with vegetable fat, beef stock, white pepper and salt.

Serve warm as is or with ilaxa wild greens or isityu meat stew for a more extravagant Xhosa meal.

For a summer dish, simply omit the beans. Once the samp is cooked through cool and serve with amasi fermented milk.

INEMBHE is the by-product of cooked samp, it's the liquid or sauce remaining. It is believed to possess special powers that make babies strong. It's also enjoyed as a casual drink or beverage snack between meals.

Xhosa cuisine: Umngqusho onee mbhotyi (samp and beans). Model wearing traditional Shweshwe skirt and Ingcawe blanket.

Umphokoqo onamasi
crumbly maize porridge with fermented milk

Umphokoqo, also known as umvubo, is cooked ground maize producing a crumbly maize meal porridge. It's slow-cooked, and the result, a maize meal dish with a thin golden-brown crust. It's served cold with fermented milk for lunch or dinner on hot days. However, the crust is removed and served separately or reserved for breakfast the following day.

This is one of my favourite dishes and can be found across many indigenous cuisines. Its local nickname is "African salad", and it's the only "salad" that you'll find in Xhosa cuisine. The name, a result of it being served cold.

The fermented milk (amasi) is served with it on the side. It's never mixed before serving. As a child, I was taught that serving the amasi on the side is a sign of respect when serving elders. This allows the elders to do the mixing themselves.

As mentioned, this dish is also interchangeably referred to as Umvubo. However, the word Umvubo refers to the process of "ukuvuba or ukuvubisa", and it means combining dry food with moisture or a liquid like milk.

The difference between this dish and other variations such as pap, aka stiff porridge, is that umphokoqo uses less water. As a result, the texture is different, and it's more crumbly. Substitutions include fine polenta instead of maize meal and buttermilk instead of amasi.

Ingredients

2 ½ cups water
4 cups maize meal
1 tsp salt (level)

Unlike other methods of making maize meal porridge, the maize meal for umphokoqo is not pre-mixed with water. It is directly added to the hot water.

In a pot, bring the water and salt to a boil.
Add maize meal to the boiling water and close the pot without stirring. Keep covered for about 8-10 minutes.

Open the pot and stir until the maize meal is well incorporated, forming tiny lumps. Cover and cook on low heat for a further 30 minutes and remember to stir every 10 minutes. This step is essential for creating that crumbly texture.

The bottom will catch a bit, forming the thin golden-brown crust associated with this dish. The crust itself is enjoyed separately with tea for breakfast the following day. Nothing goes to waste.
 Serve umphokoqo cold and enjoy with (amasi) fermented milk or fresh milk.

Quick guide to popular Xhosa cuisine

BREADS
Coal baked bread (umbhako)
Fried bread (amagwinya)
Steamed bread (isonka samanzi)

SIDE VEGETABLES
Melon (umxoxozi)
Mushrooms (amakhowa)
Pumpkin (ithanga)
Squashes (oosenza)

SNACKS
Chicken feet (amanqina enkukhu)
Pumpkin slices and fire roasted pumpkin seeds (amaceba ethanga neentanga zethanga ezosiweyo)

WILD EDIBLE GREENS (umfino)
Dandelions (irhawu)
Elephant tree leaves (igwanisha)
Nettles (ihlaba)
Prickly pear (itolofiya)
Pumpkin leaves (imithwane)

4 Cape Malay cuisine

Recipes inspired from the Western Cape region.

Cape Malay cuisine is bold in flavour and vibrant in colour. It is a fusion of traditional South African dishes with

influences from Southeast Asia. The flavours are contrasted, sweet, with savoury and mildly spiced.

Popular Cape Malay spices include mild masalas, cinnamon, cardamom, cloves and the ever so present turmeric, coriander, and cumin. These spices are usually combined with sweet and tangy apricot and raisin flavours, like in the dish bobotie. Bobotie is a spicy meat dish with raisins.

On cold winter days, bredies, which is slowly cooked meat and veggie stews, or mild flavoured curries with a slightly sweet finishing note, are cooked and enjoyed in many South African homes. Mild curries are served with sambals or pickles and chutneys.

During Easter, Cape Malay pickled fish, served with hot cross buns, is a traditional seasonal dish prepared and enjoyed by many.

Cape Malay desserts like koesisters have also become entrenched in South African culture.

This cuisine's warmth and balanced nature make it an all-time South African favourite, as you will see by the recipes from Chef Mo, aka Monicia Horne.

Pickled fish   Koolkos   Split pea soup   Malay Roti
Malay chicken curry   Koesisters

From the chef

Mo aka Monicia Horne

Born and raised in Cape Town and as the story goes with many coloured folk, I grew up coming to know the classics of Cape Malay food. As a child growing up, the food I ate was the same foods my parents consumed growing up, when it could be afforded.

Though I embarked in a food and nutrition course to further my knowledge in food, I still cook the same dishes I was brought up with.

It was only at 23 years old that I was enrolled at a university to study Food Science and Nutrition. After much confusion about deciding what to study, it was my obsession with watching cooking and culinary-related shows that piqued my interest. I would buy food magazines to try out new recipes, google the odd method and try my hand, with great pride, at creating dishes that were never part of my upbringing. Being an avid foodie, it was obvious that I should learn more about the art of food.

But why Food Science and Nutrition? I really wanted to attend a university, as I had experienced attending a college before. It turns out that CPUT (Cape Peninsula University of Technology) was the only university that accepted my age exempted application. My application was accepted, and I was granted my third choice of study: Food and Nutrition. My first 2 choices were Radiology and another health-related study - how uncanny! I was elated and relieved to be accepted. When I started attending lectures, I could not be more grateful to God for placing me in a course of study that I enjoyed. It blew my mind.

I then became keen to know about the media space. I had dreams of imagining myself as a food editor for a magazine. Needless to say, it happened, and I got to work at the magazine titles that I imagined myself working for.

I then pursued television, my current manifestation of where I want to be as I continue dreaming and believing in bigger dreams for myself.

It is in my television career that I became known as Chef Mo.

Thank God I'm not a Radiologist!

An Easter tradition

Pickled fish is an Easter Good Friday tradition in the Cape Malay community and one that's taken seriously. To illustrate this, I'll paint a picture of our family tradition.

We gather at my mom's house, and each brings our own variation of pickled fish. It's then served with dozens of hot cross buns.

There are variations to the recipe, for example, when it comes to the fish of choice; some people prefer hake, others prefer yellowtail or a combination of these two. Another popular choice is deboned snoek fish and, for those who like to splurge, kingklip fish.

Other variations include the vinegar for pickling, some people prefer using brown spirit vinegar, and others prefer white spirit vinegar. I use either, depending on the availability in my pantry.

I've adapted my recipe based on taste tests of previously tried methods and many cryptic telephone conversations with my mom. Her recipe, despite me hoping that she would eventually spill the beans, remains her secret.

Pickled fish

Ingredients for the fish

3-4 fish fillets descaled
1 cup flour
1 tbsp seafood spice
1 tbsp fish masala
salt and pepper
½ cup oil for shallow frying

Method for the fried fish

Ensure that all scales are removed from the fish fillets.

On a plate, mix the flour, seafood spice and fish masala, and then season with salt and pepper.

Coat the fish fillets in the seasoned flour.

Now heat the oil in a pan and shallow fry the fish fillets until golden brown in colour on both sides.

Set the fried fish aside.

Ingredients for the pickle

3-4 onions, sliced
2 whole cloves
2 allspice berries
1 tbsp fennel seeds
2 cardamom pods bruised
1 tbsp curry powder
1 tbsp roasted masala
1 tbsp fish masala
¾ cup brown / white spirit vinegar
3 tbsp brown sugar
a sprinkle of salt
1 cup of water

Method for the pickled fish curry sauce

Heat a glug of oil in a saucepan and saute' the sliced onions. Add a pinch of salt. This will help the onions to sweat and cook quicker. Give it a good mix and allow to cook for 2 minutes whilst stirring.

Add in the whole spices, and then add the curry powder, roasted masala and fish masala. Stir well to combine and cook for a minute.

Separately mix the vinegar and sugar together before pouring it into the sautéed onions. Season with salt. Give it a good mix, then top up with 1 cup of water. Allow simmering for about 20 minutes. Taste for seasoning. Balance the flavours by adding a little bit more sugar if the pickle is too sour or some vinegar if it's too sweet. Finally, remove the pickling sauce from the heat.

Break the fish up into chunks and add it to the pickling curry sauce. Allow the fish to sit in the liquid for a couple of hours or overnight before serving. This ensures that the flavours permeate. Serve at room temperature.

Koolkos

cabbage stew

While growing up, Cabbage stew wasn't exactly a family firm favourite. Although I loved my mothers' cabbage stew, my brothers, on the other hand, loathed cabbage.

My mom would make this dish mainly when the cabbage was in season, buying it from street vendors. Her stew, in its simplest form, was my favourite. It is one of those meals with a high nutritional value, and it stretches well for budget-conscious cooking.

This dish could also easily be enjoyed as a vegetarian option by omitting the meat. However, if you prefer meat, beef short ribs or any long stewing meat on the bone complements the flavours.

The secret of its great flavour is slowly simmering the chopped onion and garlic. The timing of adding the cabbage is also important. Too late, and it will be too crunchy.

Ingredients

2 tbsp vegetable oil
500 g beef short ribs, sliced thick with bones in
2 medium onions chopped
3 cloves of garlic chopped
2 cups chicken stock
3-4 potatoes cut into chunks
1 large cabbage shredded
salt & pepper to taste

Heat oil in a large saucepan or casserole. Add the meat pieces and brown on all sides. Remove from the pot and set aside covered.

In the pot, add in the chopped onion and cook until translucent. Season with a pinch of salt and continue to cook until the onions until golden brown in colour.

Add the garlic and then the meat with its juices. Season with salt and pepper. Cook for a few minutes, then pour in the chicken stock. Give it a good mix and allow it to cook for about 20 minutes.

Add the potato chunks and cook for a further 10-15 minutes. Once almost all the liquid is reduced, add in the cabbage and cover the pot with a lid until the cabbage has slightly wilted.

 Season with salt and pepper and give it a good mix. Allow cooking for 10-15 minutes longer.

Once the meat and potatoes are tender, dish up the cabbage stew with steamed rice. Yum!

Cape Malay cuisine

Koolkos (cabbage stew) — *Cape Malay cuisine*

Cpae Malay cuisine: Pea soup

Split pea soup

This is a very hearty, budget-friendly soup that is often made on rainy days. Typically in my family, when it rains and storms in Cape Town, you can visit any of my aunt's homes, and they would have a pot of soup simmering away on the stove. So I've adopted that tradition.

There are many different versions of this soup. Popular choices are to use the 4 in 1 soup mix with pearl barley, lentils, split peas and another grain. Also, by using beef bones in this recipe, it creates a sort of bone broth that adds to the depths of flavours. The bones and meat can be left out for a vegetarian option.

Like my mother, I also make split pea soup with a smoky twist!

Ingredients

200g streaky wood smoked bacon, diced (optional)
1 pkt (500 g) of dried split peas
300 g beef bones (optional)
1 onion, chopped
2 cloves garlic chopped
1 leek sliced
2 sticks celery chopped leaves reserved
2 carrots grated
2 small turnips grated
salt and pepper to taste

Heat a large pot with a glug of oil and brown the bacon until crispy. Remove from the fat and keep aside. In the same pan add the beef bones and allow them to brown slightly.

Next, add in the chopped onions, garlic, leeks and chopped celery and give it a good mix. Allow sautéing for a few minutes.

Add in the grated carrots, turnips and some of the chopped celery leaves. Season with a generous pinch of salt and pepper and add in the dried split peas. Mix until all the ingredients are well incorporated.

Add water until all the ingredients are covered and allow it to simmer, with a lid closed, until the split peas are tender.

In the last 5 minutes of cooking, stir in the smoked bacon bits.

Serve the soup in a bowl with a garnish of chopped celery leaves you reserved earlier.

Malay roti

Roti is a traditional dish typically made in every coloured family household or community. It's been around long before my existence and is part of the Cape Malay heritage.

It's almost honoured as a celebration meal. Often seen on the menu at birthdays, wedding anniversaries, family gatherings and even funerals. The recipe is also passed down from generation to generation.

My mom, though, has never made roti from scratch. It's instead shop-bought or gifted by an aunt or relative who has mastered the art of golden, crispy, flaky rotis. My mom, however, does enjoy cooking, and she has a knack for making traditional curry. Still, I think she may not have the patience for the lengthy process of roti making. She also dislikes spending long hours in the kitchen baking, just like me.

Serve with chicken curry.

Malay chicken curry

The curry recipe that I make, at least once a week, is my version. It too will be passed down to my future generation.

Typically, tomatoes are not added to our curry, but for me, it adds richness to the gravy and taste. The taste, with roti, is even more rewarding of the roti making process itself.

Ingredients for Malay Roti

2 cups flour
pinch of salt
170 ml water
100 g butter
1 tbsp oil for frying

Place the flour and a pinch of salt into a bowl and mix together. Add the water and mix until a dough starts to form. You might need to add more water if the dough appears too dry and not coming together. If the dough is too wet, add more flour.

Now knead to form a soft dough and then allow it to rest.

Place the dough onto a floured or oiled surface. Roll it into a log shape and cut the dough into portions of 8 or so. (Depending on how big you want them).

Now, roll a dough piece out into a circle shape, then spread it with butter. Once complete, roll it into a sausage or shell-like shape and set it aside. Repeat the process with the remaining dough pieces and allow to rest.

Heat a tablespoon of oil in a flat pan. Roll out the rotis into a circle shape and fry in the heated pan on each side until golden brown.

Fold and serve with curry.

Ingredients for chicken curry

2 tbsp vegetable oil
1 onion, chopped
8 curry leaves
2 cloves garlic, chopped
1 thumb-size ginger, grated
1 tbsp roasted masala
1 tsp chicken masala
1 tsp garam masala
4 chicken breast fillets/ deboned chicken thighs, cut into cubes
1 medium tomato, grated/ chopped (optional)
300 ml chicken or vegetable stock
fresh coriander leaves to garnish

Heat the vegetable oil in a saucepan. Add in the chopped onion and the curry leaves and sauté for a few minutes.

Add in the garlic, ginger and the spices and cook for another minute.

Add in the chicken and tomato (optional) then mix well together until well combined.

Pour in the stock and allow to simmer on medium to low heat until, uncovered, until the chicken is cooked through.

Garnish with fresh chopped coriander and serve with warm roti. This recipe also works well with lamb, beef or even just vegetables.

Koesisters

When it comes to baking, a science that needs practice to improve, I have very little patience. This is a trait that I seem to have inherited from my mom, and although it's rare for me to bake, there is an exception, namely koesisters.

For me, the syrupy, delicious, and addictive taste brings back fond memories of Sunday mornings after church. The koesisters, freshly made and still warm, were made by "motjie" (a colloquial word for the Muslim aunty on the Cape Flats) and served with a cup of tea.

When I moved to a more urbanized area, the aunties were nowhere to be found, and so I've had to make my own koesisters. But it's worth the effort. The recipe can be adjusted to personal taste.

Ingredients

5 cups cake flour
1 tbsp ground ginger
3 tbsp aniseed powder
1 tsp baking powder
1 tsp salt
1 packet dried yeast
2 tbsp cinnamon powder
1 tbsp cardamom powder
750 ml oil (for deep frying)
300 ml boiling water
250 ml cold milk
50 g margarine
4 tbsp brown sugar
1 egg

In a bowl, start sifting all the dry ingredients together.

In a separate bowl, add the boiling water and margarine. Let the margarine melt. Once the margarine has melted, add the sugar and mix.

Then add the cold milk and mix together.
Whisk 1 egg and then add it to the sifted dry ingredients.

Add the milk mixture to the dry ingredients and mix with your hand. At this point, the dough will be sticky, and that's what you want. Don't be tempted to add more flour.

Pour some oil on your hand and then rub it onto the sticky dough. Cover the dough with cling wrap and then put in a warm place to rise about 1 to 2 hours or until double in size. You do not need to knead the dough.

Shape into oblong shapes.

Deep fry on medium heat until golden brown. Drain on paper towels.

The syrup ingredients

2 cups water
2½ cups sugar
4 cardamom pods (elachi)
2 cinnamon sticks
2 cups desiccated coconut

Combine all the ingredients in a pot and bring to a boil. Let it cook for 10 minutes or until a bit sticky, and the sugar is dissolved. Lower the heat.

Now, dip the koesisters in the syrup for 40 seconds or until evenly coated with syrup. Once covered with syrup, arrange on a plate, sprinkle with desiccated coconut and serve.

Cpae Malay cuisine: Koesisters

KOESISTERS
A syrupy, delicious and addictive taste.

5 Afrikaans / Boere cuisine

Recipes inspired from the regions of Western Cape, Gauteng and Limpopo.

The word "Boerekos", directly translated, means "farmer's food". Although not all Afrikaans speaking South Africans are farmers, the term is synonymous with Afrikaans cuisine.

The cuisine can be described as country-style food characterised by big, bold meaty, starchy, filling and comforting flavours. A typical boere-plate would consist of "vleis, rys en aartapels". That is meat, rice and potatoes with the addition of "groente", (vegetables) like "boontjies" (green beans), pampoen (pumpkin) and "soetpatats" (sweet potatoes).

Boerekos is renowned for its meaty dishes, which is evident in South African barbecue known as braaivleis. Potjiekos (pot-stew) is another example of a meaty dish prepared in a three-legged cast-iron pot over a fire. A typical potjie consists of meat and vegetables combined.

These two dishes have become a phenomenon across South Africa, and Afrikaans speaking people pride themselves in the techniques of preparing braaivleis and potjiekos. In addition, "roosterkoek," a fire-roasted bread, is often served with braaivleis and potjiekos.

Biltong, a South African style of cured meat, is also a favourite. It is dried meat similar to beef jerky and made from beef and game.

Boerekos is comfort food at its best! Koos Myburgh has included some of his all-time favourites.

Tamatie (tomato) bredie   Begrafnisrys   Nico boer's braai rib-rack of lamb   Fiela's groenboontjies met aartapels   Malva pudding

From the chef

Koos Myburgh

I was privileged to have grown up in the foothills of the Helderberg mountain. We lived on the outskirts of a tiny village called Raithby in the Stellenbosch district.

During my childhood I can identify three distinct cooking influences.

Our family cook was Fiela Hartzenberg, the master of the wonderful old Aga stove. She baked the most delicious crusty loaves of bread and probably the crispiest roast potatoes for Sunday lunch. Fiela ruled the kitchen wooden spoon in hand but was always keen to encourage my involvement in the process.

My Mother Helena Myburgh was a believer in the slow cooking of hearty meals like soups and bredies. My absolute favourite was her tomato Bredie served with "Begrafnisrys."

Nico "Boer" Myburgh my father did the braai -vleis. His speciality was lamb on the spit done over open coals. A process that took five hours of constant attention. I fondly remember the vertically braaied mutton ribs and his personal favourite Galjoen fish, braaied over the coals.

Having a fair background knowledge of cooking during my youth, I continued to experiment with recipes and cooking.

My chosen career was in the events industry. This includes Event management, Event décor and of course catering for groups of people.

Nothing makes me happier than when I am cooking for the people I love.

Tamatie (tomato) bredie
recipe by my mother Helena Myburgh

Ideal for cold rainy days in the Cape, often enjoyed after slow cooking on the old Aga stove in the kitchen.

Ingredients

1 kg beef thick rib with a good layer of fat cubed.
1 kg beef shin bone in cubed leaving some meat on the bone.
3 tbsp vegetable oil
3 large onions chopped
2 tins chopped tomato
2 stalks celery chopped
1 sachet tomato paste (50 g)
3 carrots chopped
2 cups chicken stock
2 tsp salt
½ tsp ground black Pepper
½ tsp dried Italian herbs
1 tbsp sugar
4 large potatoes chopped

Warm a heavy bottom pot at high heat. Add a drop of oil and brown the meat in batches.
Remove from the oil and set aside.

In the same pot fry the onions till translucent.

Return the meat to the pot adding tomatoes, celery, tomato paste, carrots, herbs, sugar, salt, pepper and stock.

Bring to the boil then turn down the heat and simmer for two hours.

Add the potatoes and cook till both the potatoes and meat are tender.

Do not be tempted to add water. If you need more fluid add red wine or stock.

Serve with brown rice.

Begrafnisrys
funeral rice

Many years ago Afrikaans families were often spread far and wide across the country. This meant that families only got together on very special occasions often years apart. These occasions included weddings, christenings and funerals.

Great trouble would be taken and the very best of special dishes were prepared on these rare family gatherings. Hence the name begrafnisrys.

Ingredients

1 cup rice
2 ½ cups water
1 tsp salt
2 ½ turmeric
¾ cup sultanas
40 ml butter
3 tbsp honey
3 cinnamon sticks
slivered almonds for garnishing

Simmer the rice with salt and turmeric until cooked through. Rinse well and drain with a colander.

Stir in sultanas and steam over boiling water.

Melt butter, honey along with cinnamon sticks and stir butter mixture into rice.

Garnish with cinnamon sticks and slivered almonds.

Afrikaans cuisine

Nico boer's braai rib-rack of lamb

Ingredients

1 large lamb rib
1 lemon juiced
1 tbsp brown vinegar
1 clove of garlic pressed
2 tbsp whole coriander seeds roasted and finely crushed in a mortar and pestle
salt & white pepper

Cut through the ridges between the ribs so that the ribs are still in one piece resembling a hand. Cut a trellis pattern in the thick meat of the rib.

Mix lemon juice, vinegar and garlic and rub well into the ribs.

Sprinkle with salt, pepper, coriander and again rub in well.

Cover the ribs and let them marinade for an hour. Braai vertically next to the coals, turning frequently until cooked through.

Fiela's groenboontjies met aartapels
Fiela's green beans with potatoes

In the days of my childhood in the late 50's and 60's, Fiela Hartzenberg or Fielie as we fondly called her, was employed as a cook in our home. Fiela was first employed by my grandparents Rijk and Ethel Myburgh and then my mother Helena.

Fiela ruled her kitchen with a wooden spoon in her hand for close to 40 years.

Ingredients

500 g onions chopped
1 kg fresh green beans chopped
500 g potatoes diced
1 cup chicken stock
salt & white pepper

Fry the onions in butter until translucent.

Add green beans and potato and stir fry for a few minutes.

Add chicken stock and cook until the vegetables are well cooked and the stock is absorbed.

Add white pepper and adjust the seasoning.

Add another dollop of butter and give it a good stir to break up the vegetables a bit before serving.

Serve as a side dish.

Malva pudding
by Maggie Peppler

The story told by a restauranteur; Michael Oliver. The article and recipe shared by her son Dave Peppler.

In the mid-1970's I met Maggie Pepler. She lived in Stellenbosch then and had worked for a while at Lanzerac, the country-house hotel. She had also worked in the South African Embassy residences in London and Paris. Maggie is a fabulous cook and to be invited to her home for a meal is an experience that will last with me for a lifetime.

Almost 30 years on I can still remember the lamb chops she served with cherries. Food seemed to come out the tips of her fingers with consummate ease. She has a great and mischievous sense of humour, and things she said in 1970's still bring a little warm giggle and a smile to my face.

In 1978 Maggie - who had the original recipe for malva pudding- came to work for me at Boschendal Restaurant while our head chef was on holiday. I asked Maggie to teach us how to make this delicious traditional hot pudding and it has appeared on the buffet at Boschendal Restaurant every day ever since- for more than a quarter of a century.

There are many versions of this recipe as people have added a variety of other ingredients such as banana, apple, and even caramelised condescend milk! This is the benchmark Malva Pudding recipe and uses Maggie's original measurements in a 250 ml cup.

Ingredients for Malva pudding
For the dessert you will need:

1 cup flour
1 tbsp bicarbonate of soda
1 cup sugar
1 egg
1 tbsp apricot jam
1 tbsp white vinegar
1 tbsp melted butter
1 cup milk

For the sauce you will need:

½ cup cream
½ cup milk
1 cup sugar
½ cup hot water
½ cup butter

Pre-set the oven to 180 C.

Using butter, grease an ovenproof glass or porcelain dish approximately 30 cm x 20 cm. Do not use any aluminium, enamel or any metal container for baking the pudding.

Cut a piece of aluminium foil to cover the dish while the pudding is in the oven and grease it well with butter on one side.

Sift the flour and the bicarbonate of soda into a bowl and stir it in the sugar.

In another bowl beat the egg very well and add the remaining ingredients (excluding those of the sauce) one by one beating well after each addition.

Using a wooden spoon, beat the wet ingredients into the dry ingredients and mix well.

Pour the batter into the prepared baking dish and cover with the foil greased side down.

Bake for 45 minutes in the pre-set oven until well risen and browned. Add another 5 minutes without the foil if not sufficiently browned.

If not sufficiently baked, the pudding will not take up all the sauce, making it stodgy inside.

When the pudding is almost done, heat the ingredients for the sauce, ensuring that you melt all the sugar and butter.

When the pudding is done, remove it from the oven. Take off the foil and pour over the sauce. The pudding will absorb it all.

Serve hot, warm or at room temperature. Warm is best with a little thin cream.

Afrikaans cuisine

6   *The San way of life cuisine*

Recipes inspired by the regions of Western Cape, Eastern Cape, Northern Cape, and Northwest Province.

A historical depiction of the San way of life can be seen in many rock paintings and etchings in various parts of Southern Africa. They are found mainly in caves and rock shelters and are believed to be some of the oldest known examples of human art. For example, a cross-hatching drawing in ochre on stone, discovered approximately 300 km east of Cape Town in Blombos cave, is dated 73000 years ago. It is believed to be the earliest known drawing to be done by a human.

San paintings and etchings depict hunters, hunting scenes, animals and half-human half-animal hybrids, thought to be medicine men. These works of art are a historical record of the way of life and an illustrated history of modern human evolution.

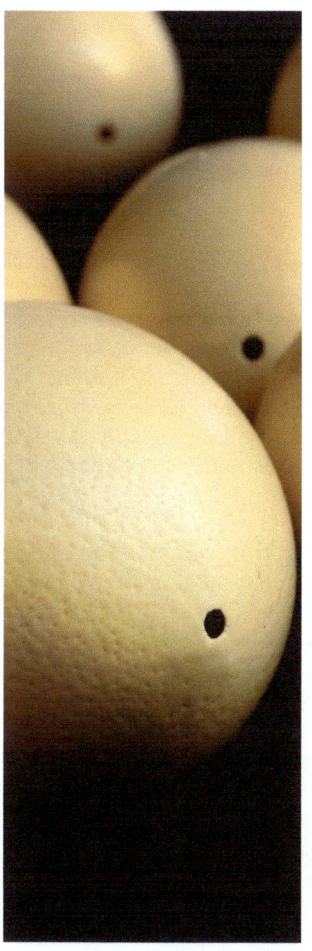

The San way of life is a deeply rooted philosophy of living in harmony with mother earth. Having conscious respect for the foods provided by her, their nourishment, and medicinal properties. This belief extends to all aspects of San way of life, including their cuisine and even their way of eating.

Eating is a process with its own rules. The San believe that they do not just eat, but rather, eat with the timing of nature in mind. The method of eating should be slow. It shows gratitude to mother earth, it is a sign of respect to the ancestors for all the living lessons of real long life and the long years granted. On the other hand, eating fast may also cause death.

The cooking methods used by the are basic, either boiling or simply, as with meat, immersing it in fire. No salt or spices are added.

Meat, such as porcupine, is held in high regard and is believed to possess healing properties, especially its stomach. Meat is portioned and eaten fresh, and the rest is dried for later consumption in soup. The San also eat their food raw sometimes.

It is also common to mix dried fruit and dried vegetables into one dish. Although wild fruits, berries, plants, leaves, bulbs, and insects are more common than vegetables.

Fruits and seeds like an African melon (tsama) and watermelon, which grow liberally in the wild, are also enjoyed.

In recent times, food is prepared as most cultures. They add more vegetables to their diet but still indulge in the San way of life whenever the opportunity presents itself.

The San recipes are from Chef Q, aka Craige Garneth Beckett.

From the chef

Craige Garneth Beckett

My name is Craige Garneth Beckett. I am a Bushman born in Johannesburg raised in the Northern Cape and reside in KwaZulu-Natal Durban South Africa.

My story begins with a grandmother who loved medicinal herbs and plants and a grandfather who taught me medicinal purposes of brandy and vodka and how to make my own alcohol.

My grandparents also taught me about different plants and their nutrients, how to hunt and gather as a way of life.

The food we ate was mostly prepared by my grandmother who taught me how to cook the Bushman way. From time to time I would pick up cooking tips from her friends in the community as well.

My grandmother cooked traditional fire food, including game or wild animal meat, plants, & wild fruits from the forest. This type of food isn't a cuisine but more of a way of life. The Bushman Way of Life.

I later on learnt the conventional way of cooking, from my time in Durban. Luckily some of the supermarkets now sell venison and ostrich these days, in that way I can still get to enjoy some of the game flavours I grew up with.

I still eat Bushman food when traveling around South Africa in places such as the Northern Cape.

This, whenever an opportunity to hunt is permitted and when I'm gathering medicinal plants. I also gather edible plants which form part of indigenous diet that I'm used to.

Unfortunately my food experience and adventure got altered for life from a trip to the dentist 8 years ago. I now suffer from trigeminal neuralgia a chronic pain condition that usually affects the nerves called trigeminal in ones face, in my case, I suffer from IAN (Iatrogenic Alveolar Nerve Damage). As a result, my cooking life now suffers a great deal as I cannot taste and smell most spices and salts.

On the plus side, this condition has allowed me the opportunity to travel Africa and Southern Africa healing people. It has inspired me to look deeper into healing finding plants that can alleviate some of my facial pain and ailments in others.

I would sometimes go as far as drive into dangerous places to work or heal, hiking in mountainous areas to find medicinal plants that alleviate pain.

This condition has taught me to be fearless and not allow pain to control my life even though I experience pain daily. Instead, I have learnt to use it for the good and the upliftment of others. I don't allow limitations to define me.

Tripe and maas meal in one
Flat bread
Porcupine stomach soup

Additional note

Q, as he is fondly known, also does a lot of community work. One of which is a campaign called Project Mantis Remote Assistance and Rural Youth Development. Lead by himself, he and his team do medicinal plant-based prevention treatment and cure remedies.

They also make cannabis oils and medicinal products for homoeopathic medicines and provide workshops to encourage the community to grow their own plants. They also teach about food security and provide sustainable development goals workshops. A project that is currently on hold due to financial challenges.

He also supports fund-raising projects for good causes. For example, in 2020, he walked from Graaf-Reinet to Cape Town and back, raising funds for reusable sanitary towels for indigenous teenage girls and their women seniors. The project stands at 3000 sanitary towels donations to date. This is his way of alleviating some of the challenges experienced by abused women in the Western Cape. The NGO is called susters4life.

In addition, Q has also started a Youth Exchange called Indigi. This program will teach rural youth sustainable living and medicinal plant culture. This will also include teaching alternative healing, agroecology, and natural farming practices. The objective of Indigi is to safeguard the youth from falling into street life. Moreover, it creates the opportunity for youth to partake in camps every school holiday.

Non-alcoholic organic home-made beverage
Dried fruit and veg pot mix

Tripe and maas meal in one

Although this dish is prepared in one pot, it will be separated and served in parts once cooked. Sheep tripe or gemsbok tripe is usually used with other organ meat such as the intestines, liver and heart added.

In a village consisting of elders, middle-aged elders and children, the elders and children will get served the softer parts of the tripe. Additionally, the elders will also get gravy and part of the intestines. The hunter-gatherers only get the liver and heart.
It's also believed that this dish helps heal stomach related problems.

Ingredients

1. 5 kg sheep or gemsbok tripe
1.5 kg intestines, liver and heart (optional)
1 bunch wild onions
2 litres maas (fermented milk) enough to cook the tripe

Place all the ingredients in a large pot and simmer in low heat until the tripe is cooked through about 4 hours. (No salt or spices are added).
The dish is then served in parts as described above.

Additional note
Dried Tripe: We also use dry tripe and chew on it as a snack that keeps hunger pains away. We believe that the sheep's tripe contains nutrients that help to sustain energy.

Flat bread

Ingredients

500 g flour
1 ½ cup maas (fermented milk)

Warm the fermented milk in a pot.
For the dough, measure the flour into a bowl. Then add the warm fermented milk to the flour while mixing.
Once the dough has formed, develop the gluten by stretching the dough with your hands.
Divide the dough into the number of flatbreads required. Flatten each piece of dough and then bake over the fire coals for about 3 minutes on high heat.

Flat bread *San cuisine*

Porcupine stomach soup

A porcupine is held in high regard in the Bushman Culture. Female porcupines are regarded as our ancestors and as healers. We believe this, because they are easier to find than male porcupines and they only eat herbs; we also believe they are the best medicine.

We hunt porcupines using tall sticks to poke holes into them and drive them out from under the ground. A spear is also helpful when they try to flee.

We then remove the quills and gently remove the insides. Then, depending on how far we are from the village or the camp, we may roast and eat it. Alternatively, we coal-burn it to preserve it as padkos (food for travelling).

The porcupine's stomach with its contents then gets dried. Still full of healing herbs, bulbs and roots. The sometimes-poisonous herbs found in its stomach are already processed, making it safe for human consumption. These herbs are believed to heal the immune system, balance any blood disorders, decrease cancers and many other illnesses.

Wild vegetables such as amadumbe or tsamma melon are added. These days potatoes or sweet potatoes are added.

Ingredients

Cooking time (+- 9 hrs)

1 female porcupine stomach fully dried
1 litre water
2 amadumbe or ½ tsama melon cut into chunks (optional)
½ cup home-made vegetable stock (made from local edible plants and herbs)

It is important to start cooking the soup first thing in the morning as the soup takes long to cook.

Start by cooking the stomach meat with water until it's tender and the water has reduced into a sauce. Then add the amadumbe or tsamma melon (if being used).

Add the vegetable stock and cook for another 45 minutes on low heat until the vegetables are cooked.

serve with flatbreads

Non-alcoholic organic home-made beverage

A modern beverage for when I'm in the city

Ingredients

1 carrot
1 pear
1 pricky pear peeled
5 cannabis leaves
a sprinkle of quinine spice
Indian or tonic water to top up the drink

Extract the juice using a juicer, then top this concentrate with a glass of Indian tonic or soda water. Sprinkle quinine spice and serve.

San cuisine

Dried fruit and veg pot mix

"This is the type of food I, as a Bushman, eat when I'm in the city".

Ingredients

250 g mixed berries and raisins dried
100 g dried ripe tomatoes
1 large onion chopped
1 spoon garlic chopped
1 spoon ginger chopped
1 fresh curry leaf
100 g pumpkin seeds
2 tbsp olive/ coconut oil (substitute with water for the bushman way).

Put all the dry fruit and vegetables into a pot or frying pan and let it braise for 5 min.

Once the onion softens, and the raisins and berries have plumped up, the meal is ready.

San cuisine

Dried fruit and veg pot mix

Tradtional hand-woven Zulu baskets

Historical grinding stones

7 Southern Sotho cuisine

Recipes inspired from the regions of Free-State and Gauteng.

Sotho speaking, Southern-Sotho or Basotho people, are proud of their traditional cuisine. A cuisine that is influenced by the historical necessity to preserve food due to migration.

The Basotho can be distinguished by their traditional attire of colourful printed blankets, called (seanamarena) and woven hats called (mokorotlo). They travelled from Lesotho, spreading across South Africa. Many Basotho settling in the Free-State Province.

A necessary requirement for travelling was the preservation of food for the journey. Therefore, the Basotho used methods of food preservation, including drying staple grains like sorghum, millet, maize, and wheat. In addition, they used fermentation for other dishes like Sorghum beer (nyekoe) and fermented sorghum porridge (motoho).
Bread making is something that the Basotho are incredibly passionate about. Traditional bread, like (bohobe), uses wheat flour, salt, a starter and water. Sugar was only added to recipes in more recent years.

Bread was and still is usually made in a cast iron pot on the coals, but other methods, like steaming, are also used. Leqebekoane is an example of steamed bread, often served with favourite greens like (morogo) amaranthus leaves.

One of the recipes from our Basotho Chef Mosa Matasane is pounded beef brisket, slow-cooked. It's a must-try, very flavourful recipe and a cooking technique also often used with meats including chicken and goat.
A cuisine worth noting and exploring.

Monepolana   Nyekoe   Mohalikoane   Lekhotloane   Lepu

From the chef
Mosa Matasane

I am a proud Mosotho woman named Mosa Matasane, whose name later changed to Makanetso Mohloai in 2018.

I'm the eldest of two girls and a mother to a baby boy.

I grew up in Mokhotlong District, one of the most remote places in the mountains of my lovely country Lesotho. I attended school there but later moved to Maseru with my family. This was due to my father's transfer as a police officer.

All the moving to different parts of Lesotho took its toll on the whole family. However, there are perks to the madness. I took the move as an opportunity to explore and learn more about the Basotho traditions along with the Basotho way of life.

Every time we settled somewhere, our sense of normalcy at home seemed to prevail quickly. I would watch my mom preparing meals for our family all the time. One of my fondest childhood food memories is watching her cook motoho or fermented maize porridge/drink and other traditional dishes. This consumed me. I found myself less interested in playing with other kids outside.

During holidays, visiting my grandmother was a way of spending more time with her. I also acquired more knowledge about the Basotho way of life and got more traditional Basotho recipes.
Once I was old enough to cook on my own, I used the inspiration I got from my mother and grandma. I have watched them cook all my life. Then replicating the dishes and adding a twist of my own.

After completing high school, my parents were now more supportive of me joining culinary school. I graduated with a certificate in culinary arts. I then got the opportunity to travel to South Africa for the first time on my own. It was for an internship and to do what I enjoy most. The training was a great opportunity to meet chefs from all over the world.

Now, I'm a professional cook with more than five years of extensive experience in Southern-Sotho and Asian Cuisine.

As of now, I am in the final stages of completing the registration of "EL-ROI RESTAURANT", my very first restaurant that will be opening soon. It's an idea that I developed way back while I was still in culinary school. The idea creates employment for my community.

The idea could not have manifested at a better time. Unfortunately, many people have lost their employment due to financial challenges that employers experienced. The result of the pandemic, an inability of employers to pay employees.
I have helped many families and still continuing to do so with food parcels in my own little way.

My wish by being involved in the Rainbow Nation Cookery Guide is to use any proceeds to support a charity in Maseru. A charity that has lost most of its sponsors due to the pandemic.

Monepolana
dry maize bread

Traditionally this bread is made from dried maize kernels that are soaked in water to soften up the outer layer. The softened maize kernels are crushed using a grinding stone. During grinding, the outer layer called bran loosens up. The bran is separated from the maize by hand. The maize is then crushed into maize meal.

The maize meal would be mixed with water, or alternatively a maize starter in this case. This mixture is left to ferment overnight. Once fermented the dough will be shaped into round balls. At first one dough ball is steamed using a traditional steamer for about 12 minutes.

After 12 minutes the steamed bread is mixed with the raw dough. The bread is then steamed for the final time until cooked through.

These days store-bought maize meal is used as a more convenient way to make the same great tasting monepalana.

Ingredients

1500 ml warm water
1 kg maize meal

Starter

500 ml water
240 g maize meal

Make the starter by mixing the water and maize meal. Mix well and leave overnight to ferment. If not fermented the next day, give it an extra day or two. Once fermented, it is time to make the bread.

In a large bowl add warm water and sprinkle the maize meal. Mix well, and leave aside to cool. Once cooled, start the kneading process by adding a little of the starter at a time until the mixture resembles a stiff dough. Cover with a tea towel and leave to rise.

Once the dough has risen divide into 2 round balls known as polokoane and steam the bread until the bread becomes fragrant and cooked through.

Served with fresh or fermented milk.
Note: left-over starter can be kept and used for future bread.

Basotho cuisine: Monepolana.

Nyekoe
sorghum and bean stew

Nyekoe is a traditional Basotho winter dish, originally made from a combination of seasonally harvested sorghum grains and beans, cooked in a 3-legged pot.

The original recipe includes animal fat, but it can be replaced with cooking oil for a vegetarian option. In addition, this recipe has evolved to include pumpkin nowadays.

The version of the recipe uses dried beans soaked overnight. It's a complete meal in one and can be enjoyed warm or cold.

Ingredients

water
1 ½ cup sorghum grains
1 ½ cup sugar beans
1 tbsp animal fat or cooking oil
salt to taste

Rinse and then soak the beans overnight in about 1.5-litre warm water. The next day, discard the soaking water and rinse the beans until the water runs clear.

Bring 1 litre of water and the animal fat, or cooking oil, to a boil in a pot. Add the beans and let them simmer until tender or almost cooked.

Then add the sorghum and cook until both the sorghum and the beans are tender. Season with salt and serve warm or cold.

Mohalikoane
toasted wheat porridge

Mohalikoane is a Basotho stiff porridge made from toasted ground wheat. Historically, wheat was toasted until brown, then ground between a larger stone (lilala) and a smaller stone (ts'ilo). The grinding process was used to create either coarse or refined flour. For a more convenient recipe shop-bought whole wheat flour is used these day. Mohalikoane can be enjoyed with wilted greens (morogo) or with milk and sugar.

Ingredients

3 cups whole wheat kernels
2 cups water

Start by pan toasting the wheat in small batches, just until lightly golden and fragrant. Once all of it is toasted, switch to a food processer.

Again, process in batches a cup at a time until flowery.

In a large pot bring the water to a rapid boil. Once boiling reduce the heat to low and vigorously stir in the first cup of the wheat flour until well incorporated for 1 minute. Cover and cook for about 8 minutes.

Remove the lid and stir in the rest of the wheat flour. Stir as previously into a stiff porridge and cover. Gently cook the porridge for another 20 minutes stirring every 10 minutes to prevent any lumps.
Serve warm with (morogo) wilted wild greens or milk.

Basotho cuisine: Nyekoe (sorghum and bean stew)

Lekhotloane
bashed beef

Lekhotloane is a uniquely Basotho meat dish; it is made by cooking meat until well done and falling off the bone. The cooked meat is then pounded with a wooden mallet (lesokoana) until it resembles shredded or pulled meat. It has a stringy texture yet is also minced.

Beef is the most common meat, but lamb and chicken are also used for this dish. It's usually served with wild spinach (morogo) or fermented dumplings (leqebekoane). Other alternative accompanying dishes include mash potatoes mixed with wild spinach (morogo).

Ingredients

500 g beef brisket
2 tbsp cooking oil
1 large onion roughly chopped
½ cup water
2 tsp salt

Cook the meat until it falls off the bone, and then remove the bones.

Now shred and bash the meat with a mallet or simply use a mortar and pestle to grind and shred it. Bash the meat pieces until they resemble shredded meat.

Now sauté the onion until it's translucent in a hot pan with oil.

Add the meat and to the browned onion. Then add the water and salt. The dish is ready when the sauce becomes slightly thicker.

Serve over mashed potatoes and wild spinach or fermented dumplings and wild spinach.

Lepu
boiled pumpkin and pumpkin leaves

Lepu is a dish typically made with home-grown pumpkin and its leaves (lebolotsana). The pumpkin and its leaves get cooked together. This dish is served with a stiff maize porridge (papa).

Ingredients

2 cups pumpkin leaves
1 baby pumpkin diced
½ cup water
½ tsp salt

In a pan, add both the pumpkin and leaves. Add water and simmer over moderate heat until cooked. Add salt and serve warm or cold as a side dish with papa.

8 English cuisine
Recipes inspired from the regions of Western Cape, Gauteng and Limpopo.

Historical English kitchenware, (Clockwise l-R): Antique copper tea kettle, wooden butter churn, bread slicer, sugar scoop, butter mould.

Top: Antique British bread knives with carved wooden handle detail on a carved wooden breadboard. Bottom: Historical butter moulds.

The English language internationally has many dialects and differences, even in the interpretation of some words vary. These adaptations also apply to South African English cuisine versus traditional British cooking. The English cuisine of South Africa is rooted in British tradition but has adapted to local flavours.

The traditional British cooking styles like roasting, baking and frying have been adopted by the South African English culture. However, the local cuisine may be described as less traditional. Factors like the temperature, weather and influences of other South African cuisines have all contributed to this.

An example of this may be a traditional British Christmas menu, ideal for winter conditions of Europe but not ideal for the hot South African climate of our festive season. Local English menus may include traditional dishes but also include lighter salads and more vegetables.

The same applies to traditional Sunday roasts, in South Africa, typically without the Yorkshire pudding.

British high tea is another example of how traditional menus have been adapted. Although high tea is not the norm, some high-end hotels still offer a traditional afternoon tea reserved for special occasions. Typically high tea showcases traditional scones, cakes, pastries and sandwiches, but locally, clotted cream is replaced with fresh cream. Also, savoury items, like quiches, are spicier, and local cakes like milk tarts are included.

From the chef

Maureen Buys

A massive Rainbow hello from me, Maureen Buys from Somerset West, situated just outside Cape Town.

I was born in South Africa to a South African 'English' Dad and an 'Afrikaans' Mom. I spent the first five years of my life in South Africa and started school in South Africa.

My Dad was in Mining, and shortly after I started school, we as a family relocated to a small remote, newly developed mining village called Mangula in Southern Rhodesia (now known as Zimbabwe). Talk about falling with one's butt in the butter, that period of my life was an experience no money could buy.

We lived in the 'Bush' wild and free. Our school had one teacher for all, and we were housed in a mining house. We went to school on our bicycles, not on tarred roads but through the bush on a path and picked fruit off the trees. Mom grew all our fruit and veggies in the garden.

Salisbury (Harare) was the main shopping centre. It was approximately a three hours drive and was a month-end weekend outing that was exciting. So many happy years enjoyed there, new food experiences, more tropical tastes, and many new cultures to embrace and learn about. The experience, priceless.

The next chapter of my life was another major move, this time even higher into Africa, Mufulira in Northern Rhodesia (Zambia). This time Copper Mining, again a multitude of new cultures, food differences and new tastes. We could travel into the Belgium Congo from Mufulira for a Sunday drive and experience a new lifestyle and totally new food trends. Mussels, huge platters of them arrived at the table steaming hot. Wow! That taste and smell could never be forgotten. I can still smell and taste them.

In those times, home entertaining was a regular weekend must-do.

My teenage years put me in contact with food preparation. Mom did most of the catering for functions at year-end, the Christmas parties for the adults and Christmas tree parties for the children.

We were all piled into the car and driven down to the mine clubhouse. We helped the moms. We were shown one platter of snacks and told to do another 50 exactly the same and don't let me dare catch you eating anything were the instructions. I loved it then and still do today.

Then a return back to South Africa, in the mid 1960's. What a change, life was busy here, cars everywhere. More routine less freedom, and a lot of don't do that or go there. I was rushed through high school, college, university etc. Then a six-year career in Mechanical Engineering, but my love of food won the day. A long career started in catering staff parties, meetings, coffee shops, canteens, functions, conventions, food shows, creating recipes for corporate companies.

My own business began with a coffee shop. I did not look for food as a career. It found me. What a journey after marriage and two lovely daughters, food became my full-time career. I started off buying my first business, a coffee shop.
I also became a member of the Chef's Association. I worked for large corporate compa-

English cuisine

nies as a Function Manager, catering to up to 4000 people daily.

My husband and I have started several businesses (16 to date), all from scratch. This included one of the first vegetable preparing companies supplying prepared vegetables to the hotel and hospitality trade. We also supplied the Blue Train (Cuisine Veggies), and then the airlines came on board. We prepared plated meals for Air Chefs, Gate Gourmet and for the first-class flights. This included supplying the prepared vegetables used for the meals served on their long haul flights. We prepared up to 4 tons of fresh veggies Monday to Fridays.

We trained staff from the surrounding area who had never worked and had never seen a potato peeler or a Ditto machine. What a joy to have had the opportunity of sharing my knowledge and giving people an income and the confidence to believe in themselves. They have become family. The staff training was my ultimate pleasure, to be able to help people without opportunities to earn a living.

I had the pleasure of meeting Pumla, a contributor to this book and the author of Pumlasfood Familystyle Cookbook. She has grown from strength to strength with her love of food. Our friendship has again introduced me to another culture in this RAINBOW Nation.

I have gained my food knowledge, not through education or cookery books, but from the hearts and hands of all the wonderful people I had the pleasure of sharing a love of food with.

Creamy scrambled eggs

British traditional tea scones

Gran's sunday lunch roast chicken

My grans' apple crumble pie

Tropical breakfast fruit salad

Additional note

Chef Maureen now mentors young chefs and entrepreneurs in the culinary industry, including Pumla Brook-Thomae, one of the contributors in this book.

Her message to all those who purchase this RAINBOW NATION COOKERY GUIDE; "May you bring joy to many when using these recipes."

Creamy scrambled eggs

Ingredients

Serves-4

**4-6 eggs
½ cup milk
salt and pepper to season
2 tbs butter
½ cup cheddar or Emmental cheese (finely grated)**

Crack the eggs into a bowl, add the milk, season to taste, then whisk well.

Heat a pan on medium heat until warm. When your pan is warm and not too hot, add the butter, and reduce the heat to low.

Whisk egg mixture again, add to the warm pan, allow eggs to set slightly, and gently fold eggs through with a spatula until all liquid is absorbed.

Remove from heat and sprinkle eggs with cheese before serving.

Serving suggestions;
Freshly sliced tomatoes or avocado or finely grated biltong for a South African twist or crispy bacon bits if you prefer.

British traditional tea scones

British traditional tea scones are a typical English tea-time treat and a breakfast component in the English culture.

Ingredients

Makes 6 scones

**120 g self-raising flour
125 g butter
140 ml milk
pinch of salt
2 tsp baking powder**

Preheat oven at 220 C.

Put the flour, baking powder and salt into a bowl and rub in the butter. Add the milk, stir well, then turn out onto a floured board and knead lightly.

Pat into an oblong shape.

Using a scone cutter, cut the scones to the desired size, place on a baking sheet into a hot oven 425F / 220 C / Gas 7 for 10-15 minutes until the scones are golden brown.

English cuisine: British traditional tea scones.

Gran's Sunday lunch roast chicken

The Sunday roast chicken recipe has stayed the same for many years in our household. It's my granny's roast chicken recipe. Although we have experimented with modern ground spices, marinades, and sauces, we all agree, we want to stick with gran's roast chicken.

Ingredients

1 whole chicken
1 celery stick chopped into chunks
1 large carrot peeled and chopped
1 leek washed trimmed & chopped
1 sprig of thyme
10 sage leaves chopped
salt and pepper

Preheat oven at 180 C.

Brush the chicken inside and out with melted butter and herbs, if using. Season generously with salt and pepper.

Season the veggies and place them into a casserole dish alongside the chicken. Close the casserole dish and roast until the juices of the chicken run clear for about 1 hour.

After an hour, remove the lid and continue roasting the chicken for another 15 minutes to crisp up the skin.

Total cooking time 1 hour 15 min for a bird with the nett weight of 1.5 kg and less cooking time for a smaller bird.

Sunday Lunch roast chicken — *English cuisine*

My grans' apple crumble pie

Ingredients

125 g margarine (room temp)
250 ml castor sugar
500 ml cake flour
5 ml baking powder
1 egg
410 g sliced pie apples
Sprinkle of ground cloves or cinnamon (Optional)

Preheat oven at 200 C.

Cream margarine and sugar until light and fluffy. Whisk in egg, then fold in dry ingredients. (Do not beat). Bring together by hand to form a soft dough.

Lightly spray a pie dish with cooking spray and press half the dough into the pie dish. Careful not to pile the dough too thick. Top the dough with apple slices or cut the apples into bite sizes if you prefer. Coarsely grate the remaining dough over the pie and sprinkle with a hint of ground cloves or cinnamon.

Bake at 200 C/400F Gas 6 for 15 minutes then, reduce the heat to 180 C and bake for an additional 45 minutes until crispy on top.

Insert a skewer to see if the apples are cooked.

Serving suggestion:
Serve warm or at room temperature, drizzled with custard or ice-cream.

Tropical breakfast fruit salad

Made with fresh fruit (of which some was grown in our garden) diced and served in a bowl.

Ingredients

½ pawpaw/papaya peeled and de-seeded
1 mango peeled and diced
1 banana sliced
1 orange (juice squeezed over the fruit)
2 granadillas (halved pulp spooned over diced fruit)
honey to sweeten (optional)

Mix all the ingredients into a big bowl and serve.

English cuisine

Apple crumble pie

Groundnuts in Tsonga hand-woven basket

Tsonga hand-woven basket

9 *Tsonga cuisine*
Recipes inspired from the Limpopo region.

The Xitsonga tribe, located in Limpopo and other parts of South Africa, are known for their culture filled with fun, energy, colourful attire, love for farming and creativity. Creativity that can be seen in their craft skills like woven baskets.

Like many African cultures, weaving is an integral part of Tsonga culture. An art form that developed from a utility need, associated with food collection, preparation and storage of foods. It is a complex and time-consuming art form, traditionally perfected by women, using available resources like grasses and fibres. The Tsonga are famous for their distinctive geometric designs, dramatic patterns and herringbone pattern rim.

The Tsonga are also well known for their farming and agricultural skills and farm crops like sorghum, millet, cowpea, monkey peanuts, amaranthus and amadumbe. This, forming the basis of their traditional cuisines with the addition of meats, like chicken, goat, beef and mopani worms.

The traditional Tsonga recipes from Chef La Bumbu, aka Xiluva Charles Ngobeni, include exotic flavours like mopani worms, monkey peanut flavoured porridge (xigugu) and dried cured meat with nuts (xiridza).

Tsonga cuisine is described as being very tasty, nutritious, and very clean flavoured.

Guxe   Vuswa bya dini   Xigugu   Matomane / Matomani
Xiridza

From the chef
Charles Ngobeni

I am Xiluva Charles Ngobeni, from Waterval, a township in Limpopo. The name "Bumbu" is a nickname given to me as a young boy, meaning "chubby". It refers to my stature and my love of eating.

Sesi Putu, my grandmother, is the one who taught me how to cook. She insisted I start cooking, which I dreaded. However, she was determined, and she would tell me how hunger would kill me if I didn't know how to cook for myself. So I learnt how to cook. She really inspired me and laid a perfect foundation for my cooking.

From then, I started experimenting on my own, which was exciting. I started playing around with flavours adding a little bit of this, a little bit of that, a bit of sweet in savouries until I obtained a flavour I liked.

This transition felt normal as my family consisted of great cooks. For this reason, I never saw a need of going to culinary school or attending cooking classes.
My sister Mapula Elsies Rampo, whose name I better mention lest I get into trouble, influenced my cooking. She is the one who helped me refine my cooking and also taught me baking.

As a child, when I was out of line, unlike other kids who were grounded, my punishment was to cook for the family. This was my sister's type of punishment.
I now realise that the punishment was there to ensure that I got cooking time and training in the kitchen. This trick flattered me and simply meant the family loved my food.

The food I cook and enjoy has always been traditional food. It's still my favourite food to eat.
Cow head (skobo) or (wa teng wembe), a cow's head recipe variation with peanuts, is my favourite dish to eat. It's served with (yellow pap) polenta. Also, I am never caught without wild edible greens (morogo) in my fridge. These are the dishes that shaped me. Most of them are what you will find in my house and as part of the menu at Chef La Bumbu's Restaurant.

When I was approached by rotary E-Club to contribute to this book, I was sold, just based on the title alone. It aligns with my brand.

At Chef La Bumbu's Restaurant, we focus on fusing traditional African food and western cuisine. The ideology of our Rainbow Nation.

We are South Africans, so we bring tastes instilled with art and tradition. Our red wine smothered (isishebo), a township stew cooked with wine, is an example of one of our fusion-style dishes.

Rainbow flavours are what we are all about. Celebrating the different flavours South Africa has to offer.

Additional note

Chef La Bumbu's Restaurant supports Mandela Day. In celebration of this big day in South Arica, he and his business partner started a motivational project. Their objective is to encourage learners whose behaviour is out of line.

They select 10 well-behaved learners for a prize of VIP Treatment. The learners are picked up in Topless Jeeps, brought to their restaurant, where chef La Bumbu gives an excellent dining experience.

The purpose of this exercise is to encourage good behaviour in learners. To give back, not material things or money. Chef La Bumbu says, we want to send a message to the learners that good behaviour pays. Since the last school they worked with, it has been reported that behaviour has improved at the school.

During the Pandemic Chef La Bumbu with other chefs joined forces for a food parcel initiative and provided over 30 families who were in dire nutritional need, they helped in the form of food parcels.

It is safe to say Chef La Bumbu is a man whose eyes are always on the look-out for where there is a need.

Guxe
sautéed wild okra

Ingredients

1 bundle okra pods (8-10)
½ cup monkey peanuts crushed
1 tomato diced
2 cups water boiled

Cook the wild okra in boiling water for 5 minutes then drain it.

Place the okra back into the pot and add the tomatoes, nuts and seasoning. Cook for a further 10 minutes and serve with (vuswa) maize meal porridge.

Vuswa bya dini
fermented porridge

Ingredients

500 ml warm water
500 ml cold water
500 g maize meal
sugar (optional)

In a bucket with a lid that closes properly add the warm water and maize meal. Stir to combine until smooth with no lumps. Close the bucket tightly with the lid on and leave to ferment for 3 days.

After 3 days add cold water to the fermented mixture and bring to a boil. Bring the mixture to a gentle simmer for about 10 minutes covered. Remove the lid and cook the porridge uncovered while stirring every now and then to prevent lumps. The more you stir you'll realize how thicker the mixture will become.

Once the porridge has set in about 10 minutes time, serve sprinkled with sugar.

Xigugu
peanut and corn snack

Traditionally xigugu is a snack made from roasted corn and roasted monkey nuts crushed together into a powder. Usually seasoned with salt and sugar. It is a simple recipe, however the grinding of the corn and nuts takes a long time, something most people dread these days and the reason why this dish is slowly fading away.

These days, the same results can be achieved by using a mortar and pestle, a food processor, or a coffee grinder to grind the peanuts.

The corn however, has now been replaced by shop-bought maize meal that is roasted and cooled then processed with the ground peanuts, sugar and salt into an oily paste.

Enjoyed as a snack just like in the olden days. A dish believed to bring good health and a good life to the Tsonga people.

Ingredients

3 ½ cups maize meal
5 cups of monkey peanuts
1 cup sugar
2 ½ tsp salt

Pan roast the nuts until lightly golden in colour and then allow to cool down overnight or until completely cold.

Once cooled, grind the nuts into a fine powder.

Now, pan-roast the maize meal and also let it cool down completely.

Mix the cooled maize meal, nut powder, sugar and salt and grind this mixture using a wooden crusher until it resembles an oily paste.

Enjoy as a snack or keep jarred tightly for up to a year.

Xigugu (peanut and corn snack)

Matomane / matomani
mopani worms

Matomani is a Xitsonga word referring to mopani worms, a regular feature in Tsonga cuisine and is highly prized due to their high nutritional value.

According to the health sector, Mopani worms consist of 60% high protein value. They are often enjoyed as a snack or served with pap. The following recipe is one of the popular ways of preparing matomani.

Ingredients

1 cup mopani worms washed clean
½ onion roughly chopped
coarsely grated
1 tomato
¼ cup cooking oil
½ tsp salt
1 l water

Use half of the water and simmer the matomani in a casserole for 10 minutes. Discard this water and put them back into the casserole.

Add the rest of the water, onion, tomato, and oil. Cook together until the matomani are cooked through and tender.

Add seasoning. Serve with pap.

Tsonga cuisine: Matomane (Mopani worms)

Xiridza
dried cured meat with nuts

Xiridza is similar to South African biltong or the American beef jerky. However, unlike other cured meat that is eaten as is, this dish requires cooking the cured meat with nuts. Important though, the pot you choose to use needs to have a stable and tight-fitting lid to execute this dish.

Ingredients

Serves-6

½ onion chopped
1 tomato diced
1 kg biltong cut into even bite sizes
½ tsp salt
½ cup money peanuts
1,5 litre water

On medium heat, simmer the biltong in about 500 ml water until almost all the water has evaporated.

Add the rest of the remaining ingredients, including the water, along with the peanuts. Close the pot and simmer for at least 10 minutes without stirring. After 10 minutes, stir the ingredients and then let simmer for another 30-45 minutes or until the biltong is cooked. Season and serve with stiff mielie pap.

Xiridza (dried cured meat with nuts)

10 Northern Sotho Pedi cuisine
Recipes inspired form the region from Limpopo and Mpumalanga.

The Pedi or Bapedi are traditionally self-sustainable farmers. They form part of the three sub-divisions of Sotho speakers in South Africa and Lesotho. Like most African cultures, women are usually responsible for farming and working the land. They are also the designated cooks.

Many Bapedi households produce their own food in small gardens, or a piece of land allocated to each family. They grow crops including maize and sorghum, the foundation to most of their dishes. Maize is a staple food and is eaten fresh, crushed with a grinding stone (lwala), or milled.

Popular Bapedi dishes, traditionally cooked in a three-legged pot over the fire, include maize meal porridge (thophi) mixed with a melon (lerotse). Maize is also combined with beans to make dikgobe. Fermented sorghum porridge (motepa wa mabele) or (motogo) and African Sorghum beer (tlhotlwa) are also traditional.

The preferred meats are beef, sheep and goats, along with mopani worms (masonja). These are often served with Amaranthus and African spinach (morogo), cooked fresh or dried for later consumption.

Chef Lehlogonolo Moifo has included some favourite traditional dishes, including a Pedi Morula beer.

Motepa wa mabele   Kgogo ya sesotho   Thelele morogo
Marula beer   Dikoko

From the chef

I am Lehlogonolo Moifo, born and bred in Limpopo. Raised by both my parents under the care of my grandparents in a township called Lebowakgomo. This is where my love of food started.

Sundays were always the best day of the week. I knew we would enjoy an array of colourful dishes known as "seven colours". A Sunday lunch that featured meat or chicken, a variety of veggies, salads and desserts. Our regular desserts were jelly and custard served with fresh or canned fruits.

I spent the last two years of my high school in Cape Town, living with my aunt, a great cook. Her cooking style influenced my cooking immensely, even though it never really crossed my mind to make cooking a career. Instead, I was rather fixated on working in the corporate world.

After matriculating, I studied Media Studies and Journalism. Once I completed my studies, I worked in the corporate world but continued to cook as a hobby. The compliments I got when hosting friends and family caused me to question my chosen career at the time and reignited my love of cooking.

After I decided to leave the corporate world and enrolled at Capsicum Culinary Studio. In 2018 I graduated and became a professional chef.

I am currently based in Pretoria, where I run my catering business and cater for the Government Sector and private clients. My dream is to open my own restaurant and also to offer training to aspiring cooks.

Lehlogonolo Moifo

Additional note

Chef Nolo has had a taste of community service after her mother invited her to support her Marula Community Project.

The Marula Project's objective was to empower disadvantaged communities in Limpopo. The communities received payment for the Marula fruit collected.

The production of the Marula fruits included using the flesh for wine and pickling. In addition, to the Marula are the nuts, either eaten as a snack or the oil extracted for cosmetics.

The nutshell is also processed and used for water purification.

It has been a while since the project has been active due to a lot of unforeseen circumstances.

Motepa wa mabele
sorghum meal porridge

Motepa wa mabele also known as motoho is a family favourite breakfast porridge across Bapedi culture. It is usually served with milk and sugar.

Ingredients

2 cups mabele (sorghum meal)
6 ½ - 7 cups water

Bring about 4 cups of water to the boil and add a pinch of salt.

In a bowl, mix the rest of the water with the sorghum and stir to form a paste.

Mix the paste with the boiling water and stir the mixture at 5 minutes intervals at reduced heat while it slowly simmers. Allow simmering for 15-20 minutes.

Serve with milk and sugar to taste. This porridge makes for a nutritious breakfast.

Motepa wa mabele (sorghum meal porridge)   *Northern Sotho Pedi cuisine*

Kgogo ya sesotho
home-bred or hard-body chicken

The Bapedi believe in keeping livestock like cattle, sheep and goats for milk, meat and wool. Chickens are also kept for eggs and meat. What would a meal be without meat! We love our meat and chicken, like most South Africans. However, leafy green vegetables do feature in our meals, but chicken and meat are still preferred.

Ingredients

1 hard-body chicken plucked, cleaned and cut into 8 pieces
1 medium onion chopped (optional)
1 ½ - 2 teaspoons salt
500 ml -1 litre water

Fill your pot with water and then bring to a boil.

Add all the chicken pieces and chopped onion. Season with salt and cook on medium heat for 2 hours or until soft. Check every hour.

Serve with stiff porridge (bogobe), also known as pap.

Kgogo ya sesotho (hard-body chicken)

Thelele morogo
wild edible leaves

Ingredients

2 cups morogo
2 tsp salt
1 cup water
1 medium tomato (finely chopped)
½ onion (finely chopped)

Bring the water and salt to boil in a pot. Add the morogo and cook for 20 minutes.
Add the chopped onion and tomato. Simmer for a further 10 minutes until tomato is cooked and serve.

Marula beer

The marula tree is indigenous to the Miombo Woodlands of Southern Africa. Its fruit (marula) is used in its entirety in Pedi cuisine. Here is a recipe for marula beer and marula fruit nut (dikoko).

Ingredients

10 litres marula fruit
2.5 litre water

Collect the ripe marula fruit. Remove the skin of the fruit using a butter knife and then squeeze the fruit pulp, pips and juice out into a large container such as a bucket with a lid. Once done, add water to cover the fruit.

Then using your hands, mash the fruit till the liquid becomes thick. Remove the pips and keep them for the next recipe.

Now cover the bucket with a lid and leave to ferment for 2- 4 days. Skim off the top layer of foam before bottling it. Ensure that it is sealed well and then store in a cool, dry place.

Dikoko
Marula fruit nut

The following snack is the by-product of making beer from marula fruits, it's the pips. They are collected and then left in the sunlight to dry out for 3-4 days.

This snack is usually enjoyed with family, bonding while cracking the nuts with a stone. The dried pips are sometimes kept in a tightly closed bottle for later enjoyment or cooking. A little bit of salt is optional for taste.

Thelele morogo (wild edible leaves)

11 Ndebele cuisine

Recipes inspired from the regions from Limpopo to Mpumalanga.

In South Africa, the Ndebele can be found mainly in small self-sufficient villages in Limpopo and Mpumalanga. They are renowned for art with their distinctive style using colourful geometric symbols.

Their art can be seen painted on their houses and similar designs in their clothing, beaded jewellery, blankets, and even contemporary artworks.

Originally this art form was meant as a means of communication. A visual language to express aspects like prayer, personal identity, values and marriage. The designs and patterns are based on and evolved from their authentic beadwork.

The Ndebele arts are also recognized internationally, and its popularity can be attributed to artists like Dr Esther Mahlangu. Her large-scale contemporary paintings depicting the Ndebele designs and her heritage has received global acclaim.

With regards to their cuisine and traditions, like many African cultures, the Ndebele people grow their own crops of maize and sorghum, vegetables and fruit. Maize is their staple food, and it forms the foundation of most Ndebele dishes like ground maize porridge with pumpkin (isijeza) and maize porridge (umratha).

Vegetables such as pumpkin, melon and its seeds are also added to maize to make a porridge. Many of their dishes are similar to Xitsonga.

Apparently, Ndebele men are not excited by veggies. They tend to leave them to women and even call it "women-food."

Chef Bongi, aka Bonginkosi Mahlangu, has included some favourite Ndebele recipes.

Historical beaded calabash

Isitshwala

Lintanga zekhabane thanga

Isijeza

Umphurhu

Umrhorhu

From the chef
Bongi aka Bonginkosi Mahlangu

My name is Bonginkosi Mahlangu. I'm 30 years old and from a small village called Matshiding.
It's located next to Siyabuswa in Mpumalanga.

I'm a single parent to my precious little son, and I regard myself as a naturally born chef.

I grew up in Matshiding and attended school there until I matriculated. As a child, I dreamed of becoming a chef. Unfortunately, I was the only one who perceived myself as such, as most of my family did not subscribe to this point of view.
By the time I was doing grade 10, I could be seen selling cakes to fellow students. I must say my business was well received by both the learners and teachers. My business did very well, but my parents were still not convinced though. All they wanted was for me to be a nurse. So finally, I gave in and did auxiliary nursing to satisfy my parents.

My love for pastry never left me during or after nursing. After completing nursing, I applied for a pastry position at Checkers Supermarket. I got the job and started working as a pastry chef. My managers at Checkers were impressed by my skills and how I brought change to the department. As a young employee, I got recognition for my hard work.

In 2015 I applied and got the job in another position. I started doing fine dining at an Italian Restaurant. I managed to climb the ladder and worked my way to a Head Chef position. My duties, though, were not limited to being a head chef only but rather an all-rounder. My responsibilities included everything, cooking, grilling, doing it all, but it excited me.
The chef who inspired me the most is Alfredo. He is the pizzeria owner who currently owns more than 10 restaurants in South Africa. I used to stand next to him whenever he was in the kitchen, learning from him. He later also hired chefs from Italy to train me and make me the chef I am today. His favourite phrase is, "If you listen to me, you will become very good." From him, I learnt to love doing everything in the kitchen and not limiting myself.

I currently work at a hotel as a Head Pastry Chef doing more than just pastry. My dream for the future is to open a top restaurant where I can work with equally motivated chefs in South Africa and expand into a franchise. I am working very hard to achieve those dreams as I believe nothing is impossible if you believe.

Additional note

When Bonginkosi is not working hard as a head chef, she assists in community events, offering chef advice, a chef eye, and labour at no charge.

Some of her wishes are to financially support a women's project that teaches farming to the youth in her community.

Isitshwala
stiff porridge

Like many South African cultures, isitshwala maize meal pap is also a favourite Ndebele dish. It's often served with wild greens such as those of pumpkin (umphurhu) or goat meat.

Ingredients

1 litre water
500 g maize meal
pinch of salt

In boiling water on low heat gently add maize meal in small batches while stirring until the texture becomes stiff. Simmer for about 30 minutes. Keep stirring every so often to prevent the porridge from catching and burning. Serve with meat stew or wild greens such as umphurhu.

lintanga zekhabane thanga
roasted watermelon and pumpkin seeds

Ingredients

100 g pumpkin melon seeds
100 g watermelon seeds
100 g
1 tbsp cooking oil

Heat the oil on medium heat in a pan until it's warm. Then add the seeds and roast until their colour changes to a golden brown. This takes about 10 minutes. Make sure you keep stirring so that the seeds don't burn.

Isitshwala (stiff porridge) — *Ndebele cuisine*

Isijeza
pumpkin & maize stiff porridge

Ingredients

300 g pumpkin peeled and diced
300 g maize meal
4 cups of water (approximately)

Cook the pumpkin in 1 cup of water until soft. Slightly mash the pumpkin with a wooden spoon and add the rest of the water. Simmer to a gentle boil. Once boiled add maize meal, a little at a time, and continue to stir until the mixture resembles a thick and smooth stiff porridge about 20 minutes.
Serve as is or with added butter and sugar if you wish.

Umphurhu
pumpkin leaves

Pumpkin leaves, like most edible leaves, are a favourite across the African Cuisine. The younger leaves, the better the taste and the lesser time they cook. However, it's essential to remove the outer layer or membrane covering the stalks before cooking the pumpkin leaves. A job that is tedious to some but well worth the pain. This recipe includes the addition of onions and tomatoes that is occasionally made.

Ingredients

150 g umphurhu pumpkin leaves washed
150 ml water
2 tbsp oil
pinch of salt

Simmer the leaves whole in water and oil for about 25 minutes. Once tender season with salt and serve.

Serve as a side dish to isitshwala.

Umphurhu and traditional Ndebele blanket   *Ndebele cuisine*

Umrhorhu
tripe stew

Tripe refers to the stomach section of a cow and or other ruminants. Before cooking it, take the time to properly wash any grit from this meat. Also, wash it under running tap water before chopping it into cubes before cooking.

In rural Ndebele Villages, this dish was only cooked with salt. It has evolved to include onions, tomatoes, stock powder or cubes and even spices these days.

Ingredients

500g tripe
2 litres of water
2 tsp salt

Make sure to wash the tripe under running water. Ensure that it's clean and contains no dirt. Take your time cleaning it as it often has a lot of dirt. Once clean, chop into bite sizes or bigger pieces if preferred.

Bring the meat and 2 Litres of water to a boil. Reduce the heat and simmer for about 3-4 hours. Once tender, add seasoning and simmer for another 5 minutes. Serve with (istshwala) stiff porridge.

Umrhorhu (tripe stew) served on historical Ndebele hand beaded placemat

12 Swati cuisine
Recipes inspired by the regions of Swaziland.

The Swati people are known to be proud. This is also evident in their workmanship of traditional arts, hand-crafts and attire.

The Swati crafts include baskets woven in bright colours, wood and stone carvings, glassware, candles, batik printing, beadwork, and jewellery.

Their traditional attire, called emahiya, also echoes their pride, representing the vibrant colours of the Eswatini flag.

Like most indigenous African people, they are also known for being subsistence farmers, growing maize, sorghum and raising livestock, like goats.

Swati cuisine is similar to many indigenous cuisines of South Africa. Sorghum and maize remain the foundation of a variety of meals. These two grains are prepared in various ways, including soft maize porridge with sugar beans called isitshwala. Alternatively, pumpkin is also added to maize to make sidvuvu pumpkin porridge.

Like the Xhosa, Swati dishes include samp crushed dried maize and beans. Emahewu, a maize meal fermented porridge drink, is also much the same as amarhewu. Furthermore, their traditional beer called umcobotsi, with maize and sorghum, is alike.

Ground nuts, like bambara nuts, are also popular in Swati dishes; they are added to pumpkin leaves to make umbidvo wetintsanga pumpkin leaves. Additionally, nuts are added to dried cured meat similar to biltong in a dish called umncweba.

Chef Jane Lukhele has included some of her favourite Swati dishes.

Mathapa   Umbhidvo wetintsanga   Tindlubu
Umbhatata   Umcobotsi

From the chef
Jane Lukhele

My name is Jane Fortunate Lukhele. I was born and raised in a village called Tjakastand at Nthlazatje Mpumalanga.

Most of my childhood was spent without my parents as they passed away when I was eight. I grew up under the care of my granny and aunt, and I was very close to them, especially my granny. She is the one who taught me how to cook. Her style of cooking was traditional dishes.

I completed (grade 12) at Macawuzela High School in 2013. Later I enrolled for a certificate in professional cooking as a chef at an institution called (MRTT) Mpumalanga Regional Training Trust. Sadly, while completing my studies in 2016, my granny passed on.

In 2017 I qualified as a chef and got an opportunity to work for Arcadia Hotel in Pretoria.

My passion has always been food, from watching my granny cook and grow her own vegetables. Years later, as a chef, I now do the same. I have a small vegetable patch at home. Growing my own vegetables is one of the ways I keep my granny's legacy. She loved gardening.

I love cooking, experimenting with flavours from around the world and trying out new recipes.

My aspirations in life include; to go into farming, develop a project to provide the community with jobs and nourishment and a house for the aged.

Hopefully, this project could bring revenue to fulfil a lifelong dream of mine, building a home for the aged. Unfortunately, I see many aged pensioners with no one to look after them, which leaves them uncared for and vulnerable.

Additional note

When Jane is not spending time in the kitchen, she can be found at The Drop-in Centre, a child base and drop-in community project that looks after orphans and children whose parents are at work. Jane also does similar work for the aged in Gugulethu and assists the home for the aged.

Mathapa
cassava leaves with crushed peanuts

Ingredients

Serves - 2

1 bunch cassava leaves
¾ cup water
½ cup crushed peanuts
2 tbs cooking oil

Start by thoroughly rinsing the cassava leaves until no more grit or sandy particles are left. Chop or process the leaves until pureed. Cook in boiling water for 30 minutes.

Add the crushed peanuts and stir to combine until the mixture becomes thick.

Then add the cooking oil.

Serve with sishwala siswati maize and bean stiff porridge.

Umbhidvo wetintsanga
pumpkin leaf stiff porridge

Ingredients

½ tbs onion chopped
1 bunch chopped pumpkin leaves stringy parts peeled & washed
¼ - ½ cup chopped tomato
500 g ground maize meal / ground peanuts
1 cup water
1 tbs powdered chicken stock (optional)
2 tbs vegetable oil

In a pan, on medium heat, sauté the onion for about 2 minutes and then sprinkle the salt.

Add the pumpkin leaves and tomatoes to the onion, then the ground maize meal or ground peanuts.

Top with water and leave to simmer uncovered for 20 minutes.

Add the stock powder, mix well, cook for another 15 minutes until cooked through.

Serve as a meal-in-one.

Swati cuisine: Mathapa (Cassava leaves with crushed peanuts).

Tindlubu

bambara groundnuts

Servings-4
Prep time-10 Minutes
Cooking Time -1 ½ Hours

Ingredients

2 cups groundnuts shell on
5 cups hot water
Salt

Sort through the nuts and discard the discoloured nuts and any impurities. Once done, rinse the nuts and then put in a pot with hot water and cook for 2 ½ - 3 hours until soft. De-shell and season with salt.

Serve as a snack.

Umbhatata

sweet potatoes

Traditionally sweet potatoes were cooked in the ground under fire. A hole was dug in the ground, the sweet potatoes buried, and a fire was then made above them. While they were cooking, we would be sitting around the fire, listening to stories told by my grandma.

After an hour, the hole will be dug open to check whether the sweet potatoes were cooked; if so, it was then served and shared while my grans' story continued.

This method was a night-time treat, but sweet potatoes were also served at breakfast with tea. Thus, this recipe is another method of preparing sweet potatoes.

Serves 4-6

Ingredients

1 kg sweet potatoes washed
500 ml water

In a closed pot, cook the sweet potatoes by boiling them in water for 30 minutes. Once the sweet potatoes are cooked, discard the water. Slightly cool for about 5 minutes, then peel and serve with tea.

Umcobotsi
African sorghum beer

Ingredients

5 kg maize meal
3 kg traditional sorghum (invubelo)
20 litres water

Finely crush about two thirds of the sorghum (2 kg) until powdery. Keep the additional sorghum for later use.

Mix the finely crushed sorghum with the maize meal. Then add warm water into the mixture and stir until well combined.

Let the mixture cool down completely then top up with the remaining water. Close the bucket tightly and leave to ferment for up to 2 days (in summer) and 3 days when it's colder.

After the first fermentation open the bucket. Add and mix the additional 1 kg of sorghum. Then close the bucket.

In another 2 or 3 days, (On the fifth day) take a sack and sieve the beer.

The beer is ready to enjoy.

Swati cuisine: Umcobotsi (African sorghum beer).

Index

A
African sorghum beer (Swati cuisine) 120
AMADUMBE (Zulu cuisine) 12
AMARHEWU 31
APPLE CRUMBLE PIE (English cuisine) 84

B
Bakes. See MALVA PUDDING (Afrikaans cuisine); See also APPLE CRUMBLE PIE (English cuisine)
Bambara groundnuts (Swati cuisine) 118
Bashed beef (Basotho cuisine) 74
Beans. See ISOPHU (Xhosa cuisine); See also NYEKOE (Basotho cuisine); See also UMNGQUSHO ONEE MBHOTYI (Xhosa cuisine)
Beef stew (Zulu cuisine) 15
Beer. See African sorghum beer (Swati cuisine); See also MARULA BEER (Northern Sotho cuisine); See also UMCOBOTSI (Swati cuisine)
BEGRAFNISRYS (Afrikaans cuisine) 50
Bread. See FLAT BREAD (San cuisine); See also ISINKWA SOMBILA (Zulu cuisine); See also MONEPOLANA (Basotho cuisine); See also MALAY ROTI (Cape Malay cuisine); See also UMBHAKO (Xhosa cuisine)

C
CABBAGE STEW (Cape Malay cuisine) 40
Cassava leaves with crushed peanuts (Swati cuisine) 116
Chicken. See CHICKEN CURRY (Cape Malay cuisine); See also ROAST CHICKEN (English cuisine); See also KGOGO YA SESOTHO (Northern Sotho cuisine)
CHICKEN CURRY (Cape Malay cuisine) 44
Cured meat with nuts (Tsonga cuisine) 96
Curry. See CHICKEN CURRY (Cape Malay cuisine); See also LAMB CURRY (Indian cuisine)

D
Desserts. See KOESISTERS (Cape Malay cuisine); See also MALVA PUDDING (Afrikaans cuisine); See also APPLE CRUMBLE PIE (English cuisine); See also FRUIT SALAD (English cuisine)
DIKOKO (Northern Sotho cuisine) 104
DRIED FRUIT AND VEG POT MIX (San cuisine) 64
Dry maize bread (Basotho cuisine) 70

F
Fermented porridge (Tsonga cuisine) 91
Fish. See PICKLED FISH (Cape Malay cuisine)
FLAT BREAD (San cuisine) 60
Fruit 31. See also FRUIT SALAD (English cuisine); See also FRUIT AND VEG POT MIX; See also NON-ALCOHOLIC BEVERAGE (San cuisine)

FRUIT AND VEG POT MIX 64
FRUIT SALAD (English cuisine) 84
Funeral rice (Afrikaans cuisine) 50

G
Green beans with potatoes (Afrikaans cuisine) 52
GROENBOONTJIES MET AARTAPELS (Afrikaans cuisine) 52
GUXE (Tsonga cuisine) 91

H
Hard-body chicken (Northern Sotho cuisine) 102

I
ISIGWAQANE (Zulu cuisine) 15
ISIJEZA (Ndebele cuisine) 110
ISINKWA SOMBILA (Zulu cuisine) 16
ISITSHWALA (Ndebele cuisine) 108
ISITYU SENYAMA YENKOMO (Zulu cuisine) 15
ISOPHU (Xhosa cuisine) 30

K
KGOGO YA SESOTHO (Northern Sotho cuisine) 102
KHARI (Indian cuisine) 23
KITCHRI (Indian cuisine) 22
KOESISTERS (Cape Malay cuisine) 46
KOOLKOS (Cape Malay cuisine) 40

L
LAMB CURRY (Indian cuisine) 22
LEKHOTLOANE (Basotho cuisine) 74
LEPU (Basotho cuisine) 74
IINTANGA ZEKHABANE THANGA (Ndebele cuisine) 108

M
Maize and bean soup (Xhosa cuisine) 30
Maize porridge with fermented milk (Xhosa cuisine) 34
MALAY ROTI (Cape Malay cuisine) 44
MALVA PUDDING (Afrikaans cuisine) 54
MARULA BEER (Northern Sotho cuisine) 104. See also African sorghum beer (Swati cuisine)
Marula fruit nut (Northern Sotho cuisine) 104
MATHAPA (Swati cuisine) 116
MATOMANE / MATOMANI (Tsonga cuisine) 94
Meat dishes. See ISITYU SENYAMA YENKOMO (Zulu cuisine); See also KOOLKOS (Cape Malay cuisine); See also LAMB CURRY (Indian cuisine); See also TAMATIE BREDIE (Afrikaans cuisine); See also CHICKEN CURRY (Cape Malay cuisine); See also ROAST CHICKEN (English cuisine); See also KGOGO YA SESOTHO (Northern Sotho cuisine); See also LEKHOTLOANE (Basotho cuisine); See also PICKLED FISH (Cape Malay cuisine); See also RIB-RACK OF LAMB (Afrikaans cuisine); See also MATOMANE / MATOMANI (Tsonga cuisine); See also Tripe

Mielie and bean stiff porridge (Zulu cuisine) 15
MOHALIKOANE (Basotho cuisine) 72
MONEPOLANA (Basotho cuisine) 70
Mopani worms (Tsonga cuisine) 94
MOTEPA WA MABELE (Northern Sotho cuisine) 100

N
NON-ALCOHOLIC BEVERAGE (San cuisine) 63
NYEKOE (Basotho cuisine) 72

P
Peanut and corn snack (Tsonga cuisine) 92
PICKLED FISH (Cape Malay cuisine) 38
PORCUPINE STOMACH SOUP (San cuisine) 62
Potato of the tropics / colocasia esculenta (Zulu cuisine) 12
Pot bread (Xhosa cuisine) 28
Pumpkin and pumpkin leaves (Basotho cuisine) 74
Pumpkin leaf stiff porridge (Swati cuisine) 116
Pumpkin leaves (Ndebele cuisine) 110
Pumpkin & maize stiff porridge (Ndebele cuisine) 110

R
RIB-RACK OF LAMB (Afrikaans cuisine) 52
Rice. See BEGRAFNISRYS (Afrikaans cuisine); See also KITCHRI (Indian cuisine)
ROAST CHICKEN (English cuisine) 82
Roasted watermelon and pumpkin seeds (Ndebele cuisine) 108

S
Samp and beans (Xhosa cuisine) 32
Sautéed wild okra (Tsonga cuisine) 91
Scones. See TEA SCONES (English cuisine)
SCRAMBLED EGGS (English cuisine) 80
Sorghum and bean stew (Basotho cuisine) 72
Sorghum meal porridge (Northern Sotho cuisine) 100
Sorghum meal porridge (Tsonga cuisine) 100
Soup. See ISOPHU (Xhosa cuisine); See also PORCUPINE STOMACH SOUP (San cuisine)
SPICY SPINACH (Indian cuisine) 23
Spinach and maize (Zulu cuisine) 12
SPLIT PEA SOUP (Cape Malay cuisine) 43
Steamed fresh corn (mielie) bread (Zulu cuisine) 16
Stew. See KOOLKOS (Cape Malay cuisine); See also NYEKOE (Basotho cuisine); See also TAMATIE BREDIE (Afrikaans cuisine)
Stiff porridge (Ndebele cuisine) 108
SWEET BUTTERNUT (Indian cuisine) 23
Sweet potatoes (Swati cuisine) 118

T
TEA SCONES (English cuisine) 80
THELELE MOROGO (Northern Sotho cuisine) 104
TINDLUBU (Swati cuisine) 118
Toasted wheat porridge (Basotho cuisine) 72
TAMATIE BREDIE (Afrikaans cuisine) 50
Tripe. See TRIPE AND MAAS (San cuisine); See also UMRHORHU (Ndebele cuisine)
TRIPE AND MAAS (San cuisine) 60
Tripe stew (Ndebele cuisine) 112

U
UMBHAKO (Xhosa cuisine) 28
UMBHATATA (Swati cuisine) 118
UMBHIDVO WETINTSANGA (Swati cuisine) 116
UMCOBOTSI (Swati cuisine) 120
UMNGQUSHO ONEE MBHOTYI (Xhosa cuisine) 32
UMNYANDU WEZINKOBE (Zulu cuisine) 12
UMPHOKOQO ONAMASI (Xhosa cuisine) 34
UMPHURHU (Ndebele cuisine) 110
UMRHORHU (Ndebele cuisine) 112

V
Vegeterian. See AMADUMBE (Zulu cuisine); See also UMNYANDU WEZINKOBE (Zulu cuisine); See also ISIGWAQANE (Zulu cuisine); See also KITCHRI (Indian cuisine); See also SWEET BUTTERNUT (Indian cuisine); See also KHARI (Indian cuisine); See also SPICY SPINACH (Indian cuisine); See also UMBHAKO (Xhosa cuisine); See also AMARHEWU; See also ISOPHU (Xhosa cuisine); See also UMNGQUSHO ONEE MBHOTYI (Xhosa cuisine); See also MALAY ROTI (Cape Malay cuisine); See also BEGRAFNISRYS (Afrikaans cuisine); See also FLAT BREAD (San cuisine); See also FRUIT AND VEG POT MIX; See also MOHALIKOANE (Basotho cuisine); See also LEPU (Basotho cuisine); See also FRUIT SALAD (English cuisine); See also ISINKWA SOMBILA (Zulu cuisine); See also GUXE (Tsonga cuisine); See also VUSWA BYA DINI (Tsonga cuisine); See also XIGUGU (Tsonga cuisine); See also MOTEPA WA MABELE (Northern Sotho cuisine); See also THELELE MOROGO (Northern Sotho cuisine); See also DIKOKO (Northern Sotho cuisine); See also ISITSHWALA (Ndebele cuisine); See also LINTANGA ZEKHABANE THANGA (Ndebele cuisine); See also UMPHURHU (Ndebele cuisine); See also UMBHIDVO WETINTSANGA (Swati cuisine); See also TINDLUBU (Swati cuisine); See also UMBHATATA (Swati cuisine); See also MATHAPA (Swati cuisine)
VUSWA BYA DINI (Tsonga cuisine) 91

W
Wild edible leaves (Northern Sotho cuisine) 104

X
XIGUGU (Tsonga cuisine) 92
XIRIDZA (Tsonga cuisine) 96

Glossary

A

Aartapels	The Afrikaans word for potato.	Afrikaans	52
Amadumbe	A starchy root vegetable related to the sweet potato.	Zulu	7,12,62,88
Amagwinya	A traditional Xhosa fried bread.	Xhosa	35
Amahewu	A traditional beverage of fermented maize porridge.	Zulu	9
Amakhowa	The word translates to wild mushrooms.	Xhosa	35

B

Begrafnisrys	The term translates to 'funeral rice" but refers to a yellow rice dish often serveFd at large gatherings.	Afrikaans	50
Biltong	Is the name for a South African cured dried meat.	Afrikaans	48,80,96
Biryani	A traditional Indian dish of spicy rice and meat.	Indian	18
Bohobe	A specific type of steamed bread.	Basotho	68
Boontjies	The Afrikaans word for green beans.	Afrikaans	48,52
Braaivleis	Translates to barbecue and refers to cooking meat over fire coals on a grid.	Afrikaans	48
Bredie	The Afrikaans word for "stew".	Afrikaans	36,49,50

D

Dikgobe	A traditional dish of crushed dried maize with beans.	Pedi	98
Dikoko	It's the name for the nut stone of the marula fruit.	Pedi	104

E

Emahiya	It's the name for Swati traditional clothing.	Swati	114

G

Ghee	It's a form of clarified butter used in traditional Indian cooking.	Indian	22,23
Groente	The Afrikaans word for vegetables.	Afrikaans	48
Guxe	It is a leafy green vegetable also known as Jews mallow or bush okra (Corchorus olitorius and C. tridens).	Tsonga	91

I

Idombolo	A specific type of steamed bread.	Zulu	9
Igwanisha	It's the Xhosa name for elephant tree leaves (edible wild greens).	Xhosa	35
Ihlaba	It's the Xhosa name for stinging nettle (edible wild greens).	Xhosa	26,35
Iimbhotyi	The Xhosa word for beans.	Xhosa	25
Iintanga zekhabane thanga	It's a traditional Ndebele dish with watermelon and pumpkin seeds.	Ndebele	108
Iintanga zethanga	The Xhosa word for pumpkin seeds.	Xhosa	35
Imbhikicane	It refers to a sheep or lamb's quarter.	Xhosa	26
Imbhuya	The Zulu word for wild spinach (edible wild greens).	Zulu	9
Imizi	It's a type of river reed used for weaving baskets.	Xhosa	24
Imithwane	It's the Xhosa name for pumpkin leaves (edible wild greens).	Xhosa	26,35
Impuphu	It's the name for milled dry maize grain.	Zulu	9

Indlamu	It's a name of a traditional Zulu dance performed by men.	Zulu	9
Irhawu	It's the Xhosa word for dandelion (edible wild greens).	Xhosa	26,35
Isigwaqane	A traditional Zulu stiff porridge dish with beans and maize.	Zulu	15
Isijeza	A traditional Ndebele maize porridge with melon or pumpkin.	Ndebele	106,110
Isijingi	A traditional Zulu maize porridge with pumpkin.	Zulu	9
Isinkwa	The Zulu word for bread.	Zulu	16
Isinkwa sombila	A traditional Zulu steamed cornbread.	Zulu	16
Isithwala / Umratha	A traditional Ndebele porridge of maize meal.	Ndebele	106
Isitshwala	A traditional Swati porridge of sorghum or maize.	Swati	108,110
Isityu seyama yenkomo	The name of a traditional Zulu stew made with beef.	Zulu	15
Isonka samanzi	A traditional Xhosa steamed pot bread.	Zulu	35
Isonka sombhako	A traditional Xhosa baked bread.	Xhosa	28
Isophu / Isophi	The name for a Xhosa soup like dish made with maize and beans.	Xhosa	30
Ithanga	The Xhosa word for pumpkin.	Xhosa	35
Itolofiya	The Xhosa word for prickly pear; a non-indigenous flowering cactus with fruit.	Xhosa	35
Iwala	It is the word for grinding stone.	Pedi	66
K			
Kgogo	It's the Bapedi word for a hard body home-grown chicken.	Pedi	102
Khari	It's the name of a yoghurt dip, served as a side dish.	Indian	18,23
Kitchri	The name of a traditional Indian spicy rice dish.	Indian	18,22,23
Koolkos	The Afrikaans word for cabbage stew.	Cape Malay	40
L			
Lebolotsana / Mokopu	The Basotho word for a small pumpkin.	Basotho	74
Lekhotloane	It's a traditional Basotho meat dish that requires bashing the meat after cooking it.	Basotho	74
Lepu	The Basotho word for pumpkin leaves and is also dish with pumpkin leaves.	Basotho	74
Leqebekoane	The Basotho name for a traditional steamed dumpling made with fermented maize.	Basotho	68,74
Lerotse	It's the Pedi word for melon and refers to watermelon (Citrullus lanatus).	Pedi	98
Lilala	It's the word for the larger, bottom stone used when grinding grains.	Basotho	72
Lwalwa	The word for a grinding stone used to mill both dried and fresh maize.	Pedi	98
M			
Maas	It's a dairy product of fermented cow milk.	Xhosa	60
Mala le menatlana	It's a traditional Xhosa dish made with chicken feet and intestines.	Xhosa	35
Malva poeding	It's a traditional baked sweet dessert. The word "poeding" translates to pudding.	Afrikaans	54
Marula	It's the name for an indigenous deciduous tree that bares marula fruits.	Pedi	99,104
Masala	It means a mixture of ground spices typically used in Indian cooking.	Indian	18,39

Term	Definition	Language	Page
Masonja	The Pedi word for Mopani worms.	Pedi	98
Mathapa / Matapa	It's a traditional Swati dish prepared with cassava leaves.	Swati	116
Matomane/matomani	The Tsonga word for Mopani worms.	Tsonga	94
	It is a traditional Basotho porridge made with toasted wheat.	Basotho	72
Mohalikoane	It is the name of a traditional Sotho hat.		
Mokorotlo	It is a traditional Basotho bread made with dried maize.	Basotho	68
Monepolana		Basotho	70
Morogo / Moroho	Also named wild spinach, Morogo refers to at least three edible dark green leafy vegetables, including cowpea, vegetable amaranth, and spider flower.	Basotho	6,7,8,72,74, 89,98,104
Motepa wa mabele	It's also known as Mabele sour porridge.	Pedi	100
Motjie	It is a colloquial Cape term referring to a Muslim aunty.	Cape Malay	46
Motoho	It's a fermented maize porridge drink.	Basotho	69,100

N

Term	Definition	Language	Page
Nyekoe	It's a traditional Basotho stew made with sorghum and beans.	Basotho	68,70

P

Term	Definition	Language	Page
Pampoen	It's the Afrikaans word for pumpkin.	Afrikaans	48
Papa	A Basotho word referring to a dish of maize meal porridge.	Basotho	74
Potjiekos	The word for a stew cooked in a three-legged cast-iron pot over an open fire.	Afrikaans	48
Prickly Pear	A non-indigenous flowering cactus with fruit.		35,62

R

Term	Definition	Language	Page
Roosterkoek	The Afrikaans word literally translates to grill-cake, but it refers to bun-sized bread made on an open fire.	Afrikaans	48
Roti	It is traditional Cape Malay unleavened fried flatbread.	Cape Malay	44,45
Rys	The Afrikaans word for rice.	Afrikaans	48

S

Term	Definition	Language	Page
Seanamarena	The name for a traditional colourful Sotho blanket.	Basotho	73
Sidvuvu	A traditional Swati porridge with pumpkin.	Swati	114
Soetpatats	The Afrikaans word for sweet potatoes.	Afrikaans	48

T

Term	Definition	Language	Page
T'silo	The Basotho word refers to the smaller oval hand-held stone used in grinding grains.	Basotho	72
Tamatie (Tomato) bredie	The Afrikaans name of a stew consisting of tomatoes and meat.	Afrikaans	49,50
Thelele morogo	The Bapedi word refers to a combination of wild dark leaf edible greens.	Pedi	104
Thophi	The name of a Pedi dish of maize meal porridge and wild melon.	Pedi	98
Tindlubu	The Swati word for Bambara groundnuts.	Swati	118
Tlhotlwa	The Bapedi name for traditional African sorghum beer.	Pedi	98
Tripe	The word refers to the first or second stomach of a cow or other ruminant used as food.	San	25,60,112
Tsama melon	The name of a type of melon that grows liberally in the wild of South Africa and Namibia. It is related to sweet melon.	San	57,62

U

Ubulongwe	The Xhosa word for cow dung.	Xhosa	25
Ugeme	The Xhosa word refers to a cut of meat, namely brisket.	Xhosa	25
Ujeqe	It's the name for a traditional Zulu type of steamed bread.	Zulu	9
Ukhamba	The Zulu word means calabash but also refers to a clay vessel used for brewing beer.	Zulu	9
Ulusu	It is the Xhosa word for tripe and refers to the first or second stomach of a cow or other ruminant used as food.	Xhosa	25
Umbhako	It's the Xhosa name of a traditional pot baked bread prepared over the fire coals.	Xhosa	28,35
Umbhalo	The name for traditional Ndebele blankets.	Ndebele	111
Umbhatata	The Swati word for sweet potatoes.	Swati	118
Umbhonomtsha	The Xhosa word for fresh maize.	Xhsoa	25
Umbidvo wetintsanga	The Swati name of a traditional stiff pumpkin leaf porridge.	Swati	114
Umbila	The Zulu word meaning corn or maize.	Zulu	9
Umcobotsi	Is the Swati name for traditional sorghum beer.	Swati	120
Umfino	The Xhosa word refers to a variety of edible leafy green wild vegetables.	Xhosa	7,26,35
Umgrayo	The Xhosa word for a refined maize product of crushed maize.	Xhosa	25
Umhlehlo	The Xhosa word for animal lace-fat.	Xhosa	25
Umncweba	The Swati name for dried cured meat.	Swati	114
Umngqusho	The Xhosa word referring to crushed dry maize.	Xhsoa	25
Umngqusho onee mbhoyti	A traditional Xhosa dish of samp and sugar beans.	Xhosa	25,32
Umnmyandu wezinkobe	A traditional Zulu dish of maize and spinach.	Zulu	12
Umphokoqo onamasi	A traditional Xhosa dish of crumbly porridge and fermented milk.	Xhosa	34
Umqa kajodo	A traditional Xhosa dish of maize rice and wild melon.	Xhosa	25
Umqombhothi	The Xhosa name for traditional Sorghum beer.	Xhosa	25
Umqombothi	The Zulu name for traditional African beer.	Zulu	9
Umratha	The Ndebele word for a bowl of maize meal porridge.	Ndebele	106
Umrhorhu / Maguru	The name of a traditional Ndebele tripe stew.	Ndebele	112
Umxoxozi	The Xhosa word for wild melon.	Xhosa	25,35
Uphuthu	The Zulu name for a crumbly fluffy maize porridge.	Zulu	9
Uphuthu namasi	The name of a traditional crumbly fluffy maize porridge with fermented milk.	Zulu	9

V

Vleis	The Afrikaans word for meat.	Afrikaans	48,49
Vuswa Bya Dini	The Tsonga name for a traditional fermented maize meal porridge.	Tsonga	91

X

Xigugu	The Tsonga name for a traditional monkey peanut flavoured stiff porridge.	Tsonga	88,92
Xiridza	The Tsonga word for dried cured meat similar to biltong.	Tsonga	96

www.ingramcontent.com/pod-product-compliance
Lightning Source LLC
Chambersburg PA
CBHW041548220426
43665CB00003B/59